the
MOONSHOT
Guidebook

A Launchpad to Your Higher Purpose

CONSCIOUS CAPITALISM PRESS™

Conscious Capitalism Press
www.consciouscapitalism.org/press

rtc

Round Table Companies
Packaging, production, and distribution services
www.roundtablecompanies.com

Deerfield, Illinois

Concept by Michael J. McFall
Text by Michael J. McFall, Laura Eich,
and Jeremy DeRuiter—with the help of many others

Printed in the United States of America

First Edition: April 2020

10 9 8 7 6 5 4 3 2

Library of Congress Cataloging-in-Publication Data

The moonshot guidebook: a launchpad to your higher purpose /
Michael J. McFall, Laura Eich, and Jeremy DeRuiter.—1st ed. p. cm.

ISBN Paperback: 978-1-950466-16-0

Library of Congress Control Number: 2020903755

INTRODUCTION

This workbook launches a new product line for Conscious Capitalism Press designed to support business leaders in the practical and operational aspects of leading and growing a business as a Conscious Capitalist. This workbook, and those that will follow, are curated and designed to help you put Conscious Capitalism into action for yourself, your team, your company, and the world around you. I invite you to dive into this engaging content, take inspiration from what you learn, notice what sparks your creativity and ignites your passion, and follow THAT—take what serves you and make it your own!

One of the most beautiful and genuine experiences that I am honored to see on a daily basis is the depth of commitment and support that business leaders in the Conscious Capitalism community show for one another. Conscious Capitalists around the world, in myriad industries, are showing us what it looks like to do business in the twenty-first century by demonstrating what it means to have a purpose beyond profit; cultivating their conscious leadership and culture throughout their business's entire ecosystem; and focusing on long-termism by prioritizing stakeholder orientation instead of shareholder primacy. This workbook is yet another amazing expression of the servant leadership necessary to make all of this possible. It is also the recognition that we all need a guide on the journey to building businesses that matter. BIGGBY® COFFEE exemplifies what it means to be on that journey.

So get ready to go on a wild ride full of energy, love, passion, and connection, where you will learn page by page how BIGGBY is transforming their business, every person it touches, and the world around us.

Onward together,

Amanda Kathryn Roman
Chief Innovation Officer, Conscious Capitalism, Inc.

P.S. Don't forget to share what is working for you—let's keep building the global network of business leaders dedicated to elevating humanity through business together! Visit www.consciouscapitalism.org for ways to connect and share.

guidebook
noun

guide book | \ \ 'gīd -, būk \
: HANDBOOK sense 1
especially: a book of information—for travelers.

. . . for travelers.

DEAR **FELLOW TRAVELER,**

BIGGBY® COFFEE exists to support you in building a life you love. We believe a key foundational element to building a life you love is knowing who you want to be. This book will help you start to define and refine who you want to be through the power of visioning. It will then help you establish, refine, and work toward your Moonshot—a statement of what you want your whole life to build toward—whether that's a single gigantic accomplishment or getting to a place in life where you're living your perfect day every single day. No matter your dream, visioning will help you get there.

Visioning is an exercise that walks you down a path of imagining your future. By doing the work and then sharing your vision with others, you will begin to emotionally engage your future.

Becoming emotionally attached to your future will help you commit, in the present, to making that future happen. But you can't commit to something that doesn't yet exist unless you are emotionally *immersed* in it. You have to be able to feel what it is like to be living in the place where your vision has become your reality. Therefore, you have to feel it, smell it, touch it, kick it, and play with it before you can immerse yourself in the reality of your Moonshot. Once you are there—once you have mentally teleported into your Moonshot— you have no choice but to be really excited about it, and you are driven to make it happen. You will create positive energy around your Moonshot and around your future. The power of positive energy is limitless.

We want to be very clear about what this process is supposed to do, and it starts with a question: *"Are you living a life today that is consistent with your vision and building toward it, or are you living a life that is being written for you by the circumstances around you?"* If you are allowing circumstances to control you, please let the visioning process free you from your circumstances of today and allow you to create a reality rooted in your vision for the future, which will undoubtedly help you build a life that you love.

Once you believe in the reality you have created for your future and allow yourself to live within it, you will start to see it realized. That's when you will feel and understand the power of the visioning process. Once you are in it and committed to it, there is nothing that can stop you from accomplishing your Moonshot and living a life that you love, we promise!

All the very best,

BOB FISH | Co-CEO/Cofounder of
BIGGBY COFFEE

MICHAEL MCFALL | Co-CEO of
BIGGBY COFFEE

WELCOME,
VISIONAUT

First time using The Moonshot Guidebook?
Here's some advice:

Don't agonize! There is no good or bad, right or wrong in this. It might be a little awkward at first, but working with it will smooth out the process. It is important to remember this is a living, breathing document you will come back to many times. Don't worry about getting it right; just get going. You will find the magic is in the process. Even if the vision for your future is foggy in the beginning, you will see that it will come into focus as you continue to work with *The Moonshot Guidebook*. The *most important thing* is that what you write in this book is **your truth.** Don't write something (or don't *not* write something) because of what you think others will think. This is your opportunity to create a future for yourself and then start living it!

Are you a veteran Visionaut?
Welcome back!

As you have likely discovered already, when faced with the exact same set of visioning questions that you have answered in the past, you can arrive at entirely new and distinct answers. These will add clarity and new direction to your day-to-day life!

So what are you waiting for? Jump in and play around!

Take it from the people who have done the work.

"Though I already had a general idea of my Moonshot prior to being introduced to this book, I had neglected to commit to ideas that I had in the back of my mind that would help get me there. This book has helped me to write down the vision for my life, and has provided greater clarity, peace, and faith as I walk on my path to the Moon. I look forward to going through the book again next year." / Dan Widmayer

"When I first got involved in this idea of visioning four-plus years ago, I tiptoed my way in; I definitely did not jump. If I look back, I can see that it was because I was afraid of committing to something and finding myself disappointed when it did not happen. What I have found since deciding to jump in 100 percent was that there is nothing I can't accomplish. By writing it down it makes your dream real and propels that dream into reality. I have achieved things I never would have thought possible like running a half marathon, handling much more responsibility at work, and even teaching others about visioning (that thing I was so afraid of). This stuff is power. It is rocket fuel. Don't tiptoe into it. Just jump." / Laura Eich

"For me, actually writing down my Moonshot and going through the exercise made it seem more real. I felt more accountable for getting to that ultimate goal. Using the Session Worksheets and goals (I don't care for the weekly stuff) to see what I had accomplished and checking things off really works for me. Now my Moonshot is always in the back of my mind. I am constantly thinking about the things I do and evaluating whether those things are helping to get to my Moonshot. I love that it does not set things in concrete but that it is fluid enough that I can make adjustments along the way." / Peggy Rector Fultz

"When I started with BIGGBY, I wasn't even able to frame up annual goals for myself. The culture here makes you take account of what you're capable of and then gives you the resources you need to grow, year after year. But nothing like The Moonshot Guidebook. I had done Michael Gerber's Primary Aim activity from The E-Myth, which was great, but this book takes it so much further. I developed a richer and deeper vision for my future, and then put it into action, based on the framework this book provides. I'm building a life I love, and I'm fired up, day in and day out, to take that next step toward my Moonshot!" / Jeremy DeRuiter

"My hesitation about using The Moonshot Guidebook came from the amount of time I felt I would need to commit to putting something on paper that I already kept in my head. This didn't seem efficient, and my thoughts should have been good enough. I had already done the Primary Aim activity as well, so again, good enough, right? I decided to be a team player and entertain the idea. I hit the ground running and filled out the first seventeen pages in one sitting. The experience was empowering and left me with a lift of energy and confidence about my future. Even at that point, I still hadn't fully engaged. I did the seventeen pages in the beginning but didn't take the time to commit to the priorities and tying my goals to my Moonshot, but this is when the Guidebook can really transform you. After engaging on a group level and sharing some of what I had put in my book, I was completely reengaged and energized again. Living your life each day with purpose and a tangible connection to what you want in your future is like nothing I have ever experienced. Do the work. Engage. You won't regret it." / Rebecca Vacek

"When I started The Moonshot Guidebook, I was pretty open to the whole idea. We had been working on visioning for a while and I just wanted to jump into it. All that said, after I read the intro and I got to the first page of inputs, it was still difficult. The first question I encountered was 'What do I wish my life to look like?' and I was immediately befuddled. I closed the book back up and decided to come back to it later. I had to give myself a pep talk. This is the conclusion I came to: 1. This isn't permanent, so just write; 2. This isn't graded, so just write; 3. Write whatever comes to your mind—it doesn't need to be Shakespeare; 4. Don't worry about judgment in general . . . after all, it's your life and nobody else's, and that can take any iteration you want. I came back, opened the book, and jumped in, and was very happy with myself, until I read the second question, 'What do I wish my life to feel like?' And again, I thought, 'What's the difference between this question and the first one?' Conclusion: who cares, just write! And this is the way I had to approach the whole process: I decided that overthinking is just a way of procrastinating, and if I could just get started (even when I didn't really know what I was doing), that was more important than having it be perfect. I had a lifetime for that. I have now coached eleven people through the process, and it's a wonderful gift to share." / Bob Fish

"I wasn't really sure what to expect when I started using *The Moonshot Guidebook*. I didn't think I would feel comfortable looking so far ahead, and I didn't understand the function of a tool like this in the workplace. After filling out the *Guidebook*, I was amazed to discover that I had a better understanding of the direction I wanted my life to go in and how BIGGBY COFFEE fit into that. Take it from a former skeptic—this stuff works!" / *Ian Sanwald*

"I am a futuristic person yet was terribly afraid of what the future held for me. I was worried that my hopes and dreams would never be accomplished. Here is the plot twist . . . I had absolutely no idea what my hopes and dreams were! It wasn't until I invested time into myself to nail down exactly what I wanted to accomplish in life—including the impressions I would make before leaving Earth—and then engaged in countless discussions that I truly knew what it was that I wanted. For the first time in my life, I can honestly say I am on the right path and know what steps to take to feel fulfilled now that I have these things written down. I have learned so much about myself by working through *The Moonshot Guidebook* and am engaging in these same types of conversations at home to begin planning our future together and see how we can both achieve our goals. This is such a powerful tool in your hands. Invest in yourself. Do the work. Revisit. Succeed." / *Dustyn Wynecoop*

"I didn't write anything in this book for the first few months that I had it because I was afraid of 'writing the wrong thing.' Once I realized that I could simply write what was true to me in the moment and refine it over time, that fear disappeared and I was able to make some awesome breakthroughs. My moonshot is still evolving, but I'm able to set goals each week that get me closer to where I want to be in life.

The most amazing part of visioning to me is the power of writing goals down and sharing them. When you put these things out in the world, it really does open doors and present opportunities that you may have otherwise missed. I have had people who I haven't spoken to in months message me out of the blue hours after writing their name in relation to a goal, and I've discovered that friends have similar aspirations that we now work together toward.

I'm still relatively early on my journey through all of this, but I can't wait to see where it takes me next, and I've really enjoyed helping others get started as well!" / *Dante Petrarca*

"Okay—so normally I have a five- to ten-year plan. This is one thing that my parents taught me. This document helped by directing me to put a lot more words to it, and think about the actions I need to take. It held me accountable for taking action.

I've always had the bigger picture written down, but the Session Goals made it easier to handle the bigger picture. This document simplified the whole process." / *MaryAnne MacIntosh*

"Most of my life I've been familiar with the concept of visioning. As a child, I daydreamed constantly. As a young adult, I read *The Secret* and in college I began a practice of guided meditation. It was always an option that seemed attractive but not something I engaged in as a regular practice—until *The Moonshot Guidebook*. I believe two aspects of this tool initiated my change: 1) diving deep into precisely what I want, going as far as writing out what I hope my eulogy would be, and 2) the Weekly Mission Sheets. It is an exquisite meld of future with day-to-day present reality.

The results felt as though they appeared out of thin air. Suddenly, this new artistic opportunity with this new entertainment company popped into my life and it just happen to be directly in line with my Moonshot. I had an epiphany, my first realization that this tool was actually leading to my dream beginning to manifest in my day-to-day life. I was floored, inspired, and deliriously excited. Don't get me wrong—I am still scared. I have a big dream, one that I was ashamed to tell anyone for years, one that I struggled to allow myself to believe; but it is my truth. I can accept that now, and am finally at the age of thirty-two pursuing a life I love all thanks to the power of intentional living, which *The Moonshot Guidebook* teaches and supports." / *Sarah Stark*

"When I first started working through *The Moonshot Guidebook*, I didn't really understand it or fully grasp how awesome this tool could be. I started working through it with my team because my boss assigned the work to us. When I initially started looking at the questions, I had no idea how to even begin answering them, and I had still had my doubts about the overall point of this activity. Then as a team, when we started sharing, I started to see the beauty and power, and each question brought me more fully into the process. Now, I love having these conversations with my team, my friends, and even my family members. This book has changed the way I talk about the future." / *Abby Bartshe*

You have an opportunity in front of you to take an active role in shaping your life and to reach your dreams.

HOW TO USE THIS BOOK

Welcome! I am so glad you're here!

I am a Moonshot Guide. That's my actual job title. Sounds like I know something about this stuff, huh? Well, here's the thing: that's a pretty recent development. As I write this, I am forty years old. Back on my first day of work at the BIGGBY COFFEE Home Office, Bob Fish sat me down and asked me what my goals were for my position—an entry-level part-time data entry job. I was stumped. I didn't know how to answer. I have no idea what I said, but I'm grateful that Bob didn't thank me for my time at that point and walk me back to the front door.

I had never been in the habit of establishing goals for myself. I was a hard worker, an achiever, but only because I always wanted to do my best and keep getting better. So, needless to say, when I was first introduced to the practice of visioning, I wasn't a natural at it.

When I answered questions like the ones you see in this guidebook, at first, it was really challenging. I wasn't sure if I was "doing it right." I also spent too much time worrying what others would think about my answers. But because of the culture here at BIGGBY, I kept returning to it. And each time I did, I understood more about myself, my insecurities fell away, and I started to dream in earnest.

When Laura and Mike created the BIGGBY COFFEE Freestyle Visioning Tool for us, I really fell in love with what visioning could do for me and all the people around me. So much so that I asked them if I could take over the BCFVT! Unlike the other visioning exercises I'd seen, it actually provided a structure to figure out the steps you need to take to reach your dreams. They asked us to find our Moonshot. And I did. My Moonshot (my fifth iteration) is to laugh at home every day and to die knowing that I've helped no fewer than one million people to build a life they love.

Laura and Mike graciously turned over the reins, and I was off to the races. I knew I wanted to share this work with as many people as I could. I expanded on the work they did by adding resources to make it accessible to people outside of BIGGBY COFFEE. *The Moonshot Guidebook* was born.

So, like I said, I'm a Moonshot Guide, and I got here with practice, learning a lot along the way. Here's my advice to you, especially if this is your first time doing this kind of work:

1. **Don't panic!** There is no right or wrong way to do this work. Start writing!

2. Don't worry about what others think. **Write *your* truth.**

3. If you can't think of an answer to a question—**skip it!**

4. Include **visual details**; it will make your vision more real to you. Yay, brain science!

5. **Share** what you've written with people in your life. Yes, that can be scary. But it's so powerful.

6. Use the **Flight Plan** and **Support Cards** to make personal change so you can be more effective.

7. Get to the **Climbing to the Stars** section as quickly as you can. That's where you start turning your dreams into a plan, and then you can start to . . .

8. Use the **Weekly Mission Sheets**! Every time you check off a to-do, you *know* you're one step closer to your Moonshot. You can live in inspiration *every day.*

Each time you do this work, it will feel more natural, you'll see more results, and fall more deeply in love with visioning and especially with your Moonshot!

With love and inspiraton,

Jeremy DeRuiter
Moonshot Guide, BIGGBY COFFEE
jeremy@biggby.com

CONTENTS

BEFORE YOU BEGIN

Friendly advice: there is no right or wrong way to work in this book! Pen or pencil, perfectly composed or full of cross-outs and arrows—make it yours to make it work for you!

MOONSHOT WORKSHEET

What do I wish my life to look like?

I WISH FOR MY LIFE TO HAVE FREEDOM AND IMPACT I WANT TO BE MAKING A POSITIVE DIFFERENCE IN THE LIVES OF THOSE AROUND ME. I WANT THE FREEDOM TO BE ABLE TO DO THIS ON MY TIME IN A WAY THAT ALLOWS FAMILY

What do I wish my life to feel like?

I WISH MY LIFE TO FEEL JOYFUL, FULFILLED, AND CHALLANGING. I WANT TO BE STIMULATED TO GROW WHILE BEING FULFILLED WITH MY CURRENT ACOMPLISHMENTS. I WANT TO FEEL AS THOUGH MY LIFE HAS MADE A POSITIVE CONTRIBUTION TO SOCIETY.

How do I wish my life to be on a day-to-day basis?

I WISH TO HAVE THE FREEDOM TO HAVE CONTROL OVER MY DAY-TO-DAY. I WISH TO TRAVEL AND MEET EXCITING NEW PEOPLE I CAN ENGAGE WITH. I HOPE FOR MY SCHEDULE TO BE FLUID.

What would I like to be able to say I truly know in my life, about my life?

I WANT TO BE ABLE TO TRULY SAY I MADE THE BEST OF MY LIFE I COULD. I WANT TO BE ABLE TO KNOW THAT I WAS ABLE TO HELP OTHERS BE THE BEST INDIVIDUALS THEY COULD BE. I WANT MY LIFE TO HAVE BROUGHT A LITTLE LIGHT TO OTHERS.

How would I like to be with other people in my life--my family, my [...]
my community?

I WANT TO BE GENUINE
LIFE. I WANT TO BE
OF JOY BUT ALSO A S[...]
I WANT TO BE REME[...]

How would I like people to think about me?

I WOULD LIKE PEOPLE [...]
KIND, FIERCE, BRAVE, NO[...]
STRONG, LEADER, GO-TO

Rebecca Vacek
BIGGBY COFFEE Home Office

Tony DiPietro
BIGGBY COFFEE Home Office

MOONSHOT WORKSHEET

I get emotional because I feel that my time to truly enjoy life had pass[...]

What do I wish my life to look like?

- In better health, less stress, more stability, debt free, better credit score, Financially stable, that I was ok w/ where I'm @, celebrate the victories more, that I could slowdown, Peaceful,

→ what a fall day looks like around a camp fire w/ family x friend

What do I wish my life to feel like?

A sense of accomplishment
- 2 acres on a lake - circular drive way - a lake
- Cape Cod - white w/ wood trim - a pole party "barn" - 3 Flags & a cannon - My kids could build on the property - A/an in the
- My family would be financially sound - house filled w/ loved ones
- ownership in BIGGBY - debt free - feel loved + give love ea. MOMENT of ea. day

→ real travel + love ea. moment helping others reach goals - healthy family + I

How do I wish my life to be on a day-to-day basis?

That I was proud of all my interactions w/ everyone
I cared about to act in a way where it [...] I
died they would cherish that interaction

MOONSHOT WORKSHEET | SESSION ONE

Remember: *There is no right or wrong way to do this, so long as you do it! You don't have to answer the questions in order. You don't have to fill up the lines or stay within them. Want to do your first draft on another sheet of paper or on a computer? Okay, cool! Just so long as your truth ends up in this book, you're doing great! Now, some tips:*

1. **Don't overthink the questions.** You will return to these questions again and again over the years on the way to attaining your Moonshot. This is just the starting point! If you need a little more room, use the margins.

2. **If you need a bunch of room, add a footnote** and continue writing in the notes section (page 108). For example, just put a "1" by the question, and then number your note in the back of the book.

3. **If you are married or in a committed relationship,** we recommend having each of you work through your own individual guidebook and then share with each other. You will need to be aligned on parts of your long-term vision. Dynamic conversations ahead!

4. **Need help getting started?** Watch the same presentation we shared with the BIGGBY family at our 2018 Franchise Meeting at www.biggby.com/visioning.

5. **If you get stalled out in the middle of working on the questions,** STOP thinking about it. Go for a walk. Put on some music and just listen. Change up your method. Think of your childhood—favorite memory, favorite game, best friend, etc.

6. **Feeling a little stuck?** Try browsing the examples page at the end of this section (page 18)—seeing how others have answered the questions can help you find your own answers.

7. **Feeling a lot stuck?** Like you can't see any way forward? Head to Houston, We Have a Problem for some extra advice (page 28).

8. **If you are still stuck after that, partner up with someone** in your life you can talk to about your stuckness. Just talking through it could help you find the way forward.

1) What are some skills that I wish I had?

_____

_____

_____

_____

2) What are the things I want to own that I don't own today?

_____

_____

_____

_____

3) Where would I like to live across the course of my life?

_____

_____

_____

_____

If you are already more than a week into this year, get started right away on your Weekly Mission Sheets. Even if you haven't completed your Moonshot or set goals for the session, set some very short-term goals and start building the habit of getting focused on the things that matter most.

4) Where would I like to travel?

_____
_____
_____
_____
_____

5) What do I hope to accomplish in my life?

_____
_____
_____
_____
_____
_____

6) What do I hope the people in my life would say if someone else asked about me?

_____
_____
_____
_____
_____
_____

7) What would my perfect day look like?

_____
_____
_____
_____
_____

8) What would a perfect week feel like, start to finish?

_____
_____
_____
_____
_____

9) Two years from today, how would I like to be spending my time?

The date two years from today: _____   My age, two years from today: _____

_____
_____
_____
_____
_____
_____
_____

10) What about in ten years?   The date ten years from today: _____   My age, ten years from today: _____

_____
_____
_____
_____
_____
_____
_____
_____

11) And twenty years from now?   The date twenty years from today: _____   My age, twenty years from today: _____

_____
_____
_____
_____
_____
_____
_____

12) In the last chapter of my life?

_____
_____
_____
_____
_____
_____
_____

FUEL UP

Hey! If you've answered at least a chunk, if not all, of the preceding questions, it's time to start sharing. The act of sharing is powerful. It is the fuel you will need to reach your Moonshot. When you share:

1. **Your answers become more real for yourself.** You will unconsciously begin to commit to your vision in a way that's not possible through simply writing it down.

2. Even if the people you share with don't offer feedback, simply speaking the words to another human being will help you evaluate them in real time. **You might discover new things**, or required changes, as you talk through your vision.

3. **You will create bonds with the people you share with.** If you have your authentic truth written down on these pages, you will welcome people into your life in a way that doesn't happen through casual conversation. Even years' worth of casual conversations.

Here are some recommended practices:

• If the people you're sharing with don't have a copy of The Moonshot Guidebook, let them start by browsing through it. Most people in your life don't have access to this kind of a tool. Getting their hands on it will be the first step to recruiting them to your mission.

• Read to them aloud. This is the magic behind #2 above.

• Invite the people you share with to ask you questions about what you have written. Give them time to engage after each answer you read. When they ask, "What do you mean by _____?" whether that's a word or a whole paragraph, they are helping you to refine your vision.

• If they do have their own copies and have done the work . . . you are primed and ready for a powerful experience. Sharing in this way will pull you closer together, and it means you can help each other at the work of reaching your Moonshot. Teamwork makes your dream work!

In a small group (two to four people), read through four questions at a time, per person, pausing between questions to invite feedback and questions.

After each person has read through the first four questions, move on to the next four. This sharing can be broken up across different days, or with a different number of questions, depending on how much time you have to commit to it. Just be sure each person has the opportunity to share and receive input equally.

In larger group settings, like larger teams or families, you will want to proceed question by question, person to person. Depending on how much time you have and the size of the group, you might need to limit the amount of interaction.

• Make note of any questions you get so that when you return to this work in the future, you can expand on what you have written.

• Next up is the Eulogy and the Moonshot. The exact same sharing rules apply. Get together with someone in your life and share. Sharing is creation. The people you share with will be people you care about and who care about you. They will be a crucial part of reaching your Moonshot, so get started and get them on board with you!

• When others share their Moonshot with you, record it in the Moonshot Dashboard in the back of the book (page 104). This will help you keep track of the most important ambitions of the people in your life. It will inspire you and keep you open to noticing opportunities that you can share with them to further their dreams!

WRITING
YOUR OWN
EULOGY

Or story of your life, if you prefer.

This is a thought experiment. It is the chance to capture all of the biggest moments in your life and the people who were important to you. Proceed with a sense of curiosity. This is a chance for you to explore.

Describe your funeral service or visitation, celebration of life, wake, etc., in great detail. Where is it being held? Who is in attendance?

What are they doing? What does it sound like? Is there music playing? Explain who is reading your eulogy and why. Write your eulogy word for word.

We understand that some will struggle with this assignment for a wide variety of reasons. The idea of this is to capture the story of your life—what you did, what you meant to the people in your life, and what you are leaving behind. While we think there is a clarity you can achieve when describing your own funeral and eulogy, if you prefer to write it looking forward rather than looking back, that is fine as well! End the story wherever you feel is appropriate. The important thing is to try to describe as many of the important moments across the course of your life that you can.

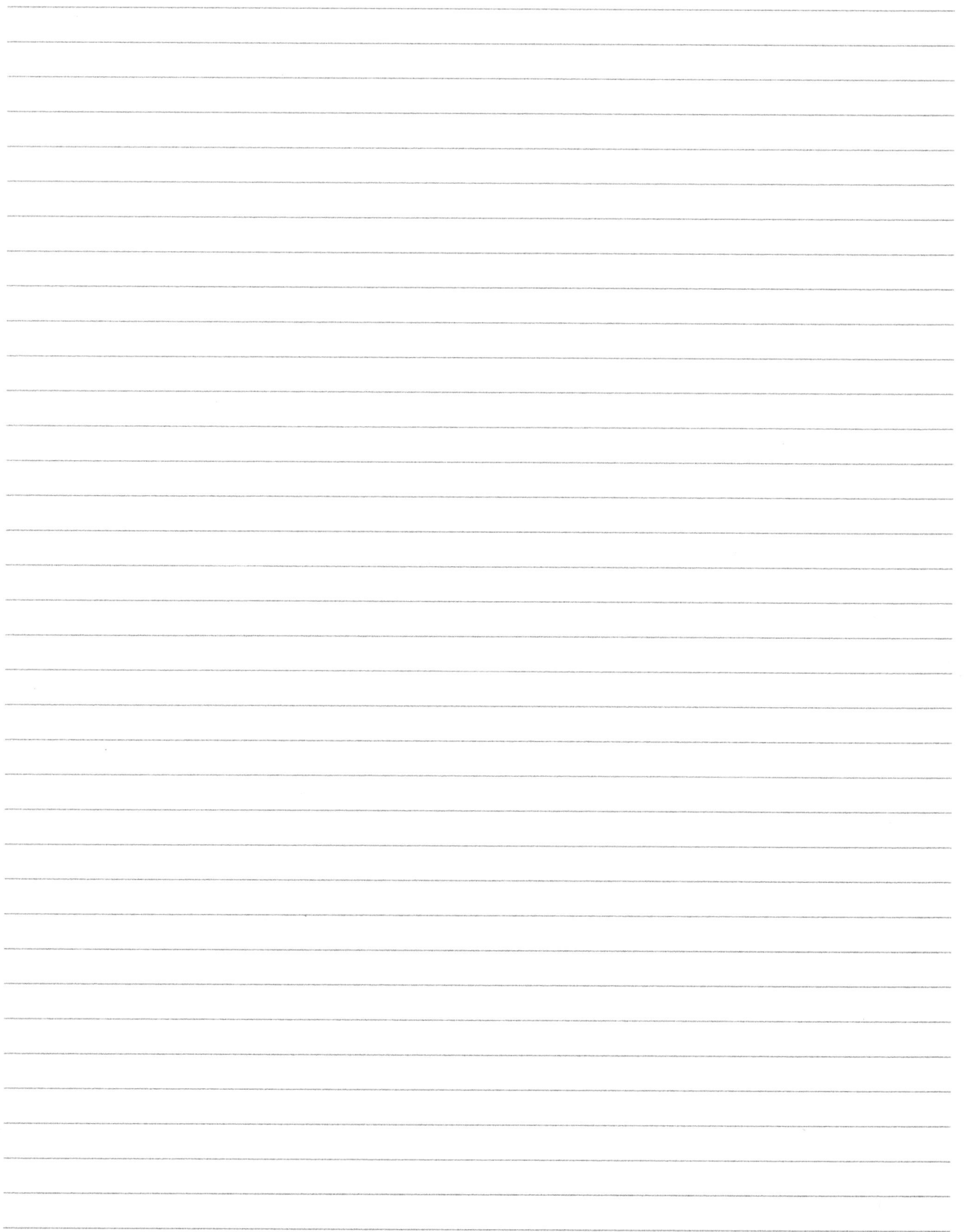

MY MOONSHOT

Reflect on what you have written in the Moonshot Worksheet and boil it down to a simple statement that sums it up for you. If you could accomplish one thing in your life, or live your perfect day every day, what would it look like? Don't forget that you will return to this and refine it over time!

_____
_____
_____
_____

DESCRIBE YOUR LUNAR LANDSCAPE

Write ten visually descriptive details below—these will help you visualize your Moonshot and emotionally connect to it. What does life look like leading up to your Moonshot? Once you have achieved it? You will continue to refine these details in Session Two, so don't agonize!

1] _____

2] _____

3] _____

4] _____

5] _____

6] _____

7] _____

8] _____

9] _____

10] _____

We would LOVE to see your Moonshot! Take a picture of this page after you have completed your answers and send it in to moonshot@biggby.com.

MOONSHOT
WORKSHEET EXAMPLES

Seeing what others have written can be helpful when creating your own Moonshot. This cannot replace the experience of sitting in a room with the people in your life and reading from your book. For now, feel free to browse the work of other BIGGBY family members to see what they found for themselves.

4) Where would I like to travel across the course of my life?

Italy, Japan, Australia, Germany, South America, Africa, the UK, Spain, Russia, NYC, Chicago, Miami, Hawaii, someplace tropical, Ventura CA,

5) What do I wish my life to look like?

Uniquely successful. My converted industrial estate is my home base with buildings for a shop, a pool, nature, and vehicle storage. I spend time travelling with friends in my airships, and promoting my brand. I have a remote property where the airship hanger is, along with other fun vehicles. I am engaged in the car community.
*what does this mean?

6) What do I wish my life to feel like?

Fun - I will enjoy every day. Successful - I won't have a single worry about money. Creative - I will be able to turn my ideas into realities. Free - I will be able to do what I want each and every day. Fulfilling - I will know that what I've built made a difference & will leave a legacy
→ what does this mean?

7) How do I wish my life to be on a day-to-day basis?

what does this look like?   evening routine

I'll kick off every day with my morning routine, but from there every day will vary. I'll pick a different vehicle each day based on my needs and mood. Regardless of where I am or what's on my plate, every day will include productivity, laughter, and fun

8) How would I like to be with other people in my life—my family, friends, business associates, customers, employees, my community?

I want to stay in touch with the people that matter to me, no matter where we are. I want to be an important part of people's lives, and I hope that people will look up to me. I want everyone to know that I am here for them if they need help. I want to be friends with coworkers & customers, and respected in my industry. I will be involved in my community and have a positive impact on it.

9) What are some of the specific things I want to learn over the course of my life?

I want to learn what it's like to have an incredibly close bond with another person, to learn how to meditate and really get something out of it, how to fly, how to run a business w/employees, how to do business internationally, how to design & build a home/shop, how to TIG weld, how to better draw or render my ideas, how to commit to decisions faster

moonshot worksheet

/13

Landmark in Livonia

4) Where would I like to travel across the course of my life?

Every State in the US. And my vacation list.

5) What do I wish my life to look like?

Structured, yet comfortable enough to let loose.
Full of love, pride in my family. Sharing
my life with that special someone. Work hard-
play harder. Get to making and checking off my
bucket list.

6) What do I wish my life to feel like?

Next to no conflict. The ability to relax and
be grateful. To take things in stride and not
take on others burdens as my own. Ability to
let go. No regrets. Fun + more freedom to do
whatever @ drop of a dime.

7) How do I wish my life to be on a day-to-day basis?

Structured mostly   coffee at sunrise
good balance of alone time and being surrounded
by the people I love. Teaching moments. Hugs
and laughter. A dog. A good book. Good food.
End of day:

8) How would I like to be with other people in my life—my family, friends, business associates, customers, employees, my community?

A role + good listener - reliable.
Someone who may not have all the
answers, but is sincere about helping, teaching,
growing with them. I want people to be able
to count on me. mostly I want people to be
proud to call me their friend.   "endless reserve"

9) What are some of the specific things I want to learn over the course of my life?

True patience. Love without worry of loss
Freedom of acceptance - that other peoples
decisions are not my burden. make my money make $
How to be healthy and fulfilled. Paddle board.
Pull a trailer. Build a fire.

moonshot worksheet

13

Heather Maynard, BIGGBY COFFEE District Manager

How do I wish my life to be on a day-to-day basis?

To invest 90 minutes in myself daily, through exercise and reading/learning. To spend time on the important, not urgent. To feel unhurried and focused. To feel productive and fulfilled at the end of the day. To spend my evenings laughing and having fun with Megan.

Jeremy DeRuiter, BIGGBY COFFEE Home Office

What do I wish my life to look like?

I want my life to look full. I want to be surrounded by my family. I want us to always be pushing each other to reach for our stars. Kind of like that out of body experience you get when you're having a good time and you're genuinely happy and you stop in the midst of it, take it in, and realize how happy you are in that moment. Exactly that.

Erica MacLeod, BIGGBY COFFEE Home Office

What do I wish my life to feel like?

Warm. Like the warm feeling you get in your chest after you take a shot of tequila. Like the warm feeling on your face in the morning when the sun wakes you. This is how the love in my life and heart will feel. The kind of happy you feel when you're drunk without being drunk. As carefree as the day when you first got your license. The feeling in your stomach the first time you saw the love of your life.

Erica MacLeod, BIGGBY COFFEE Home Office

How do I wish my life to be on a day-to-day basis?

Early start with an investment in heath (through exercise), short on tasks, long on mind time. Strong communication with a wide network of positive & growth minded people. Close out my day with family & friends.

Bob Fish, BIGGBY COFFEE Co-CEO

How do I wish my life to be on a day-to-day basis?

Wake up energized, go to work where I have a "no stress" attitude, hit the gym or some type of workout, go home in the evening to spend it making healthy dinner and then relaxing with my doggo & boyfriend."

Lily Hare, BIGGBY COFFEE Franchise Manager, Saginaw, MI

How would I like to be with other people in my life—my family, my friends, my business associates, my customers, my employees, my community?

I want to be genuine with the people in my life. I want to be positive and a source of joy but also a source of trust and reality. I want to be remembered for my real kindness.

Rebecca Vacek, BIGGBY COFFEE Home Office

How would I like to be with other people in my life—my family, my friends, my business associates, my customers, my employees, my community?

*Available	*Dependable	*An example	*Honest	*Open	*A "teacher" and a "student"
*Fun	*A cheerleader/supporter				

Meghan Atkinson, BIGGBY COFFEE Owner/Operator – Burton, Clio, and Flint, MI

How would I like to be with other people in my life—my family, my friends, my business associates, my customers, my employees, my community?

— always proud of interactions
— that I cared, I was a "multiplier"
— that I wanted to make things better
— that they all mattered to me & make me better
— that I gave 100%
— to be remembered

Tony DiPietro, BIGGBY COFFEE Home Office

How would I like to be with other people in my life—my family, my friends, my business associates, my customers, my employees, my community?

Kind, honest, loving, leader, patient, a guide, loyal, dependable, faithful to God above all.

Abby Bartshe, BIGGBY COFFEE Home Office

How would I like to be with other people in my life—my family, my friends, my business associates, my customers, my employees, my community?

I want people to know I am open (always willing to learn). I want the people around me to feel taken care of. I motivate, support, and lift others up.

Alisha Stewart, BIGGBY COFFEE Home Office

WRITING YOUR OWN EULOGY

Or story of your life, if you prefer.

This is a thought experiment. The chance to capture all of the biggest moments in your life, and the people who were important to you, and vice versa. Proceed with a sense of curiosity. This is a chance for you to explore.

Describe your funeral service, or visitation, or celebration of life, or wake, etc., in great detail. Where is it being held? Who is in attendance?

What are they doing? What does it sound like? Is there music playing? Explain who is reading your eulogy and why. Write your eulogy word-for-word.

We understand that some will struggle with this assignment for a wide variety of reasons. The idea of this is to capture the story of your life— what you did, what you meant to the people in your life, and what you are leaving behind. While we think there is a clarity you can achieve when describing your own funeral and eulogy, if you prefer to write it looking forward, rather than looking back, that is fine as well! End the story wherever you feel is appropriate. The important thing is to try to describe as many of the important moments across the course of your

I will be cremated and do not want a sad, stuffy funeral. Instead I would like my family, friends & loved ones to celebrate together. It will be a Celebration at Blue Moose (which is my favorite sports Bar. My oldest daughter Deanna will be reading my Eulogy. Thank you all for being w/ us today to celebrate the life of a loving woman, my mother, Heather. There are no lessons about how to be a great mother, we can only do our best and hope that we do it well. My mother certainly did it well!! She was a caring, supporting & loving wife, mother, grandmother, friend & mentor who loved life & the people around her. My mother was proud of all her children. I have lost my wonderful mom, adviser, mentor & friend I am so honored to have been her daughter, I will miss the amazing relationship we had. ~~But as they~~ ~~&~~ We have all suffered a huge loss. She taught us all what is really important in life: to love unconditionally, support & care for family & friends, to work hard & to always go after your dreams. We are all better off for have knowing & building a relationship with her. My mom was a huge Buckeye fan so at this time

the Battle Cry. The rest of the evening we will spend sharing our favorite stories of ~~my mom~~ her, eating & drinking & celebrating her life. Cheers!

Heather Stevenson, BIGGBY COFFEE District Manager

WRITING YOUR OWN EULOGY

Or story of your life, if you prefer.

This is a thought experiment. The chance to capture all of the biggest moments in your life, and the people who were important to you, and vice versa. Proceed with a sense of curiosity. This is a chance for you to explore.

Describe your funeral service, or visitation, or celebration of life, or wake, etc., in great detail. Where is it being held? Who is in attendance?

What are they doing? What does it sound like? Is there music playing? Explain who is reading your eulogy and why. Write your eulogy word-for-word.

We understand that some will struggle with this assignment for a wide variety of reasons. The idea of this is to capture the story of your life— what you did, what you meant to the people in your life, and what you are leaving behind. While we think there is a clarity you can achieve when describing your own funeral and eulogy, if you prefer to write it looking forward, rather than looking back, that is fine as well! End the story wherever you feel is appropriate. The important thing is to try to describe as many of the important moments across the course of your life that you can.

The brewery is packed. Both bars are open and the servers and bartenders are all hustling to keep up. A person walking in off the street wouldn't know they are joining in on the celebration of a life well lived — people are happy, animated, + enjoying each other's company — sharing stories of the person who all brought them there that day.

Our stranger off the street would see that the crowd is full of people off all ages, all walks of life. As the stranger winds his way to the bar he hears snippets of conversation in languages that sound like German, Spanish, and a language he can't quite peg, but Asian -sounding for sure.

After some time the music turns down and a middle aged man with a fantastic Scottish accent warmly welcomes the crowd. "I'm so glad to see so many of Jeremy's friends, family, and community members here tonight — it's a testament to the impact he's had. My name is ___ and I'll serve as our emcee tonight for our storytelling. I met Jeremy and Megan at a small restaurant in Edinburgh when I was just a 24 year old server. We struck up a conversation about my plans for the weekend, which turned into a much longer conversation, across weeks and years. That conversation changed my life, but for him, it was just a Tuesday lunch, out with his wife. And that's just the way he was. Effortless deep care for the people around him. I expect we'll hear that same sort of story throughout the night, and I look forward to hearing them. First, I'd like to welcome up Jonathon, Jeremy's brother.

Jeremy DeRuiter, BIGGBY COFFEE Home Office

A slender, elderly man, with a hint of a smile and sharp eyes, not dimmed by age or life joins him, hugs him, and takes the mic.

"Ah, I loved my brother. And looked up to him all these years. He said he looked up to me too, which I never quite understood, as my older brother, but, there you have it.

"You all already know this, but it's worth saying — Jeremy was all-in on life. This was a man who never had a bored minute. When he was with you, he was with you — all-in, engaged, interested, fun and funny, challenging in a good way, compassionate. His marriage to Megan is one for the story books. She's here today, and I'm speaking for her as well. They were best friends — it was so evident. Jeremy stated it as part of his Moonshot in their 10th year of marriage — to laugh at home, every day. I believe they made good on that. They reveled in each other's company, but never excluded others from that warmth and interest. They adventured together across the course of their lives making memories and friends all over the world.

"And then there was his Moonshot Institute — where the vision of BIGGBY aligned with Jeremy's personal vision. He spent years and years worth of time there, but never worked a day in his life. He loved what he did — helping people find their own Moonshot and then plugging them into a community of people who will help them accomplish it. That's part of the magic of how the Institute grew to be a multinational organization — it was powered by the shared interest and love of a community of people like Jeremy — passion-driven, and invested in making an impact for the people in their lives.

"So, while I miss him dearly, I take comfort in knowing that all of you here today loved him like I did, and are also a part of him accomplishing his own Moonshot — there's no better way to send him off than reaching your own dreams and then sharing it. Please, raise your glass to Jeremy, Megan, and a million Moonshot dreams. Cheers."

Jonathan passes the mic back to ___ who hugs him and then welcomes up the next speaker and the scene repeats itself again and again amongst the sounds of laughter, some grateful tears, and food and drink shared with family and friends.

Jeremy DeRuiter, BIGGBY COFFEE Home Office

(cont.)

MY MOONSHOT

Reflect on what you have written in the Moonshot Worksheets and boil it down to a simple statement that sums it up for you.
If you could accomplish one thing in your life what would it be?

I am a top-grossing film actor who travels the world frequently to act while balancing a joyful, healthy home life with my husband and children.

DESCRIBE YOUR LUNAR LANDSCAPE

Imagine that someone has time travelled into your future and spends time documenting your life once you've accomplished your Moonshot. Describe in vivid detail ten pictures that the time traveler will take of your future life.

1] Oscar night, I walk with joy and confidence down the red carpet in a stunning gold dress. Size 4, photography beautiful, I will win my 1st Oscar tonight.

2] It is a beautiful purple and orange sunrise in LA, slightly cool as I run towards the Hollywood hills, my body is lean and strong, my heart pure joy.

3] On the coast of New Zealand I sit in near white sand beside a bonfire holding my children, near my husband laughing, telling stories, gazing at stars.

4] It's in the 80's, bright sun, bustling European city we walk all day, me and my family staying in the beautiful architecture, art galleries, local cuisine just exploring all day.

5] I attend an international theatre festival with my husband and children seeing theatre by artist from an array of countries, come together.

6] My mother holding each of my twin girls in her arms shortly after their birth at the hospital. They have black hair and are in perfect health.

7] laying on a cabana lounge on the room of my garden patio on our roof of our Miami condo, warmed by the sun, reading a book as my children and husband swim. I can see the ocean.

8] Climbing a mountain in AZ with my children and husband, feeling strong and warmed nicely by the sun, enjoying the stunning views.

9] On a blockbuster film set, in a slinky, sexy dress about to perform a tango on screen, my lips are red, I dance flawlessly in heels and impress everyone on set.

10] I am riding a horse in beautiful natural countryside and carrying a sword, a hybrid of a beautiful Queen and fierce warrior for a blockbuster film.

We would LOVE to see your Moonshot! Take a picture of this page and send it in to moonshot@biggby.com!

my moonshot session two

69

Sarah Stark, BIGGBY COFFEE Home Office

MY MOONSHOT

at you have written in the Moonshot Worksheet and boil it down to a simple statement that sums it up for you. accomplish one thing in your life, or live your perfect day every day, what would it look like? Don't forget that this and refine it over time!

To chase adventure often, to Love unconditionally and without expectation, and to inspire others to do what they are afraid of.

DESCRIBE YOUR LUNAR LANDSCAPE

Write 10 visually descriptive details below—these will help you visualize your Moonshot and emotionally connect to it. What does life look like leading up to your Moonshot? Once you have achieved it? You will continue to refine these details in Session Two, so don't agonize!

1] A young woman stops me on the street and tells me that she read my book and chased an adventure.

2] I walk the stage to recieve my masters degree. I have the awesome responability of speaking at the ceremony. About love.

3] I sit in a rehearsal room with a wind symphony. They are rehearsing my piece. They will perform it next week.

4] I see Laura's face waiting for me at the end of the marathon. She finished way before me. I've raised the same as her, and when I cross the finish line, it is hers. To grant her wishes.

5] There are white lights all around as I say "I do" to the man I Love. My dress is simple; long. I've never had a fuller heart.

6] My list is online for all to see. Others start their own lists.

7] I hike the last few miles of a months long journey, everything is green, everything is alive. I'm alive.

8] I sign on the dotted line for a small living space in an environment that I love.

9]

10]

Brie Roper, BIGGBY COFFEE Home Office

The members of the Ray Kroc Forum—a group of BIGGBY Owner/Operators and Home Office staff—played a critical role in the development of *The Moonshot Guidebook*. Here is a sample of work from MaryAnne MacIntosh—you'll recognize this as an early iteration of the Moonshot and Lunar Landscape sheet.

Primary Aim Vision

MaryAnne MacIntosh, Owner/Operator – Alma, Cadillac, and Traverse City, MI

Please write your primary aim below:

Freedom – to travel or do what I want when I want.

Descriptive Detail #1:

I want to have 5 BIGGBY stores; Alma paid off – Caddy ½ done.

Descriptive Detail #2:

I want to have $3,000 monthly income from each store.

Descriptive Detail #3:

I want to have 3 stores by age 50. $3k each store, 5 @ $15,000 each month.

Descriptive Detail #4:

I want to have all stores open by age 55.

Descriptive Detail #5:

I want to retire and have all stores fully functional by age 56 – more detail – manage staff – not working stores.

Descriptive Detail #6:

I want to start traveling by age 60. Financial planning for family – kids. Wealth planning.

Descriptive Detail #7:

I want John to quit his job within the next 3 years – sell my house and buy a mobile home and travel.

Descriptive Detail #8:

I want to be able to send my son to school w/o having him take loans out.

Descriptive Detail #9:

I want to help my son open his stores whatever they may be.

Financial planning for business – succession planning.

BiGGHAG Visioning Tool

Peggy Rector, Owner/Operator – Lima, OH

Please write your BiGGHAG aim below:
To be financially comfortable enough and healthy enough to do whatever I want whenever I want.

Descriptive Detail #1:
Main residence on the 2nd floor of the remodeled 401 N Main St building.

Descriptive Detail #2:
Own a decked out RV for traveling.

Descriptive Detail #3:
Travel throughout the US to bicycle, kayak, cross country ski, sight see, hike, and lay on a beach.

Descriptive Detail #4:
Bicycle throughout Europe and Australia.

Descriptive Detail #5:
Celebrate and share trips and holidays with family.

Descriptive Detail #6:
Be a major influence in the revitalization of downtown Lima. Possibly owning more property.

Descriptive Detail #7:
Healthy eating for the most part while also enjoying different foods and drink.

Descriptive Detail #8:
Not working on the line at BIGGBY, but have an interest for as long as possible.

Descriptive Detail #9:
Mind still functions great. Body still works great. Live a ripe old age. Have fun everyday.

Descriptive Detail #10:
Have several vehicles to choose from to drive at any given time.

Descriptive Detail #11:
Volunteer at hospital, food bank, American Cancer Society Events.

HOUSTON,
WE HAVE A PROBLEM

This work isn't easy, especially at the very start. Getting stuck is normal—expected, even. The First Rule is: don't panic. Remember that this is only your current iteration—this plan for your life will be revised and re-revised over time. Fun fact: Galileo recognized that the moon was a planet that could be walked upon. That was 1609. How many ideas, dreams, and plans got written and rewritten before Neil Armstrong planted that flag? Just get moving and see what you discover!

Beyond that, I have some practical suggestions for the areas where people commonly get jammed up. If you find yourself stuck in a way that these suggestions don't help, please reach out to moonshot@biggby.com. We might be able to help, and if we can, we'll learn more that we can use to help future Visionauts!

Good luck!

Jeremy

I'm too young! I don't have a clue where I'm headed!

First of all, please high five this page right now. That's me celebrating with you for being here. You get to paint on a huge, mostly blank canvas, so the opportunities ahead of you are Jupiter-sized. Now, let's get on to some tips:

• Remember the First Rule. You'll do this work three times this year. AND you can always go back and add or cross out anything that you like. Write what feels right, right now!

• This is your truth. An easy trap for a young person is to want to fit into someone else's vision of what their life should be. Parents. Friends. Boss. They might be cool, but they're not you. You do you, boo.

• Journal or record yourself talking through it. Get away from all of the question prompts. Just start writing, or take a voice memo and get to talking. Describe where you're at right now and why the future seems so uncertain. Write or talk until you don't have anything left to say. Then turn the page, or start a new recording, and talk about what or who you love. What excites you right now. What makes you want to daydream. See what comes out, and you might have an answer.

I'm too old. My path is pretty much already set.

I have bad news for you. You're wrong. Sorry to disagree and all that, but that's just the truth. Tamae Watanabe climbed Mt. Everest at 73. Lt. Col. James C. Warren received his pilot's license at 87. Heinz Wenderoth completed his doctorate at the age of 97. You have a choice on how you want to be, no matter your age or circumstances.

My life is upside down. I don't even know what tomorrow looks like.

I'm very sorry, and I'm rooting for you. There are many different circumstances that can lead to a sense of a loss of control in your life. Death of a loved one. Divorce or breakup. Losing your job. Financial disaster. Illness or injury. Here are a few thoughts that I hope will help you:

• Visioning is an opportunity to regain some control. If you don't feel in control of your today, start working on tomorrow instead.

• You might do that by rewriting what has happened to you to make you feel this way, or starting with exactly where you're at and write your way back to happiness.

• Share with someone. Having someone work with you who doesn't share your perspective might open up new possibilities that you simply can't see from where you stand.

I'm happy! I don't want to change a thing!

First of all, I'm happy that you're happy! High five this page right now! That being said, I was happy as a five-year-old playing cops and robbers with sticks for guns (yes, I sound like I was born in 1910). Happy as I was, I'm really, really glad that I'm not still out in the front yard yelling "Freeze!" with a dead maple branch in hand. Just remember that your happiness, and the value you take from and contribute to life, is limitless.

YOUR FLIGHT PLAN

In our work together to build lives we love and perform at our highest level, it is critical we are all working together and coaching each other on how to perform better. No matter how good you are, you need a coach. Olympic and professional athletes have coaches. And they are better for having them.

At work, at home, in any community we are a part of, we have a role. All of these spaces offer opportunities to be coached in order to improve and get better at performing in this thing called life. If we are lucky, work can be the petri dish that we grow within and test ourselves in—an environment that provides regular feedback and coaching from people who care about us and are invested in our success. Your coworkers are your teammates. If you're lucky, they push you, they support you, and they expect you to grow.

The work we do in life is the challenge. We want to improve so we can conquer the current goals and objectives so we can take on a greater challenge tomorrow. It is the game we are all playing. It is what makes living this life rewarding and fulfilling. Ever since we were children, getting a high mark in a class, winning the science fair, or going to the state championships in sports have been the highlights. They make all of the work, the exhaustion, and the sacrifice worth the time and energy spent.

But work is work, and accomplishment is accomplishment. It is nothing more if you aren't experiencing it with others. The camaraderie on a team that accomplishes its goals is the most rewarding of all. We work together. We help each other. The team performs at higher and higher levels because of the commitment of each member to coaching others and complementing the attributes of each other daily. High-functioning teams perform at much greater heights than a group of talented individual performers looking out for their own self-interests. People learn and grow much more powerfully when they are in a group and committed to each other's development.

The hard part is knowing how to help others and for others to know how to help you. This stuff is difficult to communicate especially when working with someone who isn't on your minute-to-minute team. This is where the Flight Plan tool comes into play in our world. We want to utilize this tool to clearly and succinctly communicate with every other member of BIGGBY Nation what respective strengths, weaknesses, and developmental goals we have in order to communicate how we can help and what we need help with.

Each and every member of BIGGBY Nation—Owner/Operators, Home Office staff, Baristas, PERColators, Managers, Vendor Partners, and Fanatics—needs to be committed to helping every other member of "the Nation" in reaching their goals and ultimately their Moonshot. The Flight Plan tool is the way we all know how to help.

Please take your time with this piece. The more genuine and authentic the effort and work put into the piece, the better quality input and assistance you will receive. Also, the more effectively you will be able to help others. In the end, we are all in this together, and the more we know about each other, the better we complement each other.

FLIGHT PLAN WORKSHEET | SESSION ONE

This worksheet will help you complete your Flight Plan. It will take some time to think through in a solo setting and may even require some time spent asking others for help. Once you complete these steps, you will be left with a tool that will help you harness your strengths for the benefit of yourself and the people around you. The Flight Plan is also a guide to the behaviors that may hinder your growth and the growth of those around you. Getting aligned on your Flight Plan is a critical step in setting yourself up for best results while working toward your Moonshot.

1) So, the first step is to rewrite your Moonshot. And no, this is not even close to the last time we will ask you to do that.

_____

_____

_____

_____

The next step in creating your Flight Plan is to establish what others can rely on you for. If you haven't yet, we recommend that you read the book *StrengthsFinder 2.0* by Tom Rath. The author establishes a case for focusing on strengths rather than spending vast amounts of time and energy trying to improve where you are weak. The book includes a code that you can use online to take the StrengthsFinder test, which will provide you with your Top Five Strengths (alternatively, you can download their app and pay for and conduct the test there as well).

We have included a full list of the strengths from *StrengthsFinder 2.0*, along with our short descriptions, in the back of the book (page 107) as a reference, should you not have access to the book, app, or test.

2) Write your strengths here, along with what each one means to you:

1] _____

2] _____

3] _____

4] _____

5] _____

Take a look at your Top Five Strengths. Without using the actual words of your strengths, what do they tell you about yourself?

Are you more inclined to executing tasks quickly, influencing people, building relationships, or thinking strategically? Or are you a mix of all of them?

If your strengths fall strongly into the relationship-building category, maybe what you can be relied on for is that you could help two people who don't have these strengths to begin the process of forming a relationship? If you are especially skilled in execution, you are going to be someone who can be relied on to get things done, to make things happen. And so on.

Maybe you know you have a skill that is not directly related to your strengths but you know it could be valuable for people to utilize. Write that down in this space. People need to know what they can count on you to provide them in their work and life. If you are still unsure, reach out to several people and ask them: What do you count on me for? What do I offer that you seek me out to utilize? Do I have a special skill or ability that you recognize in me?

3) Please write down at least one thing that others can rely on you for here:

_____

_____

_____

_____

4) Now, using your Top Five as a starting point, write out what you wish your Top Ten would look like, including making changes to your Top Five if you feel they should change. Refer to the Strengths list on page 107 for help.

1] _____ 2] _____ 3] _____ 4] _____ 5] _____

6] _____ 7] _____ 8] _____ 9] _____ 10] _____

The next step in establishing your Flight Plan is to determine what your opportunities are for growth. To figure this one out, you need to seek input from others. Consider critiques from job performance reviews. Seek out advice from the people in your life who can answer the question "What can I do to bring us better results?" Spend time in self-reflection. Think about areas in your life where you know you are creating friction that is unproductive—at home, on the job, with friends or family. Take accountability for your role in those issues. Are there places or relationships in your life where you are being inauthentic? Where you are wasting your energy trying to look good? Consider the cost of that. What are you missing out on in life because you aren't showing up fully as the true you?

What do you see, or what can the people in your life point you toward?

5) These are my opportunities for growth:

_____

_____

_____

Here are some additional prompts to help you spot other areas of opportunity to work on and get support from others on:

6) What personal improvement am I working on already?

_____

_____

_____

7) What have my boss (or others) and I talked about in the past that I need additional work on?

_____

_____

_____

8) If my boss (or others) were to give me one piece of advice, what would it be?

_____

_____

_____

9) Do my past critiques suggest a theme of something that I should be trying to improve? If yes, write that here:

_____

_____

_____

10) Which parts of my work style or the way I communicate cause the most trouble? How do I frustrate people?

_____

_____

_____

Specifically, what do I need to work on to be ready for the next level of development or leadership in my life? What critiques does my boss or partner have for me? What about a peer, friend, or loved one?

11) Boss/Partner:

_____

_____

_____

_____

_____

_____

12) Peer/Friend/Loved One:

_____

_____

_____

_____

_____

_____

Understanding and communicating the things that motivate you and add stress to your life will help you get better results. If you have taken a DiSC Assessment, your Workplace Profile will be a great starting point for these answers. If not, think about the things that leave you feeling excited and hungry for more, and then the things in life that take a lot of extra energy or patience to endure.

13) If applicable, my DiSC Style is: _____

14) Motivators – What in my life or work environment motivates and excites me?

_____

_____

_____

_____

_____

15) Stressors – What are the things that stress me out or take a lot of energy from me?

_____

_____

_____

_____

_____

Congratulations! You have almost completed this step in the process. All that is left is to transcribe the information on this worksheet to your Flight Plan on the next page and then carry that information with you and use it to communicate with the people in your life for the coming session.

Don't forget to . . . _FUEL UP_. Share your Flight Plan with the people who will help you grow into who you want to be!

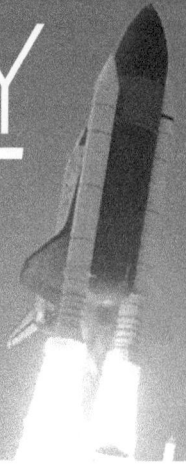

MY FLIGHT PLAN

FIRST SESSION | January–April

MY MOONSHOT:

_____
_____
_____

YOU CAN RELY ON ME TO Here are a few strengths or behaviors that you can rely on me to do consistently:

_____
_____
_____

THINGS I NEED TO IMPROVE Help me by watching for these things and letting me know when I am doing them [especially in real time]:

_____
_____
_____

TOP FIVE STRENGTHS

1] _____ 2] _____ 3] _____ 4] _____ 5] _____

MY MOTIVATORS These are the things that give me energy:

_____
_____
_____
_____
_____
_____
_____
_____

MY STRESSORS These are the things that drain my energy:

_____
_____
_____
_____
_____
_____
_____
_____

SHARABLE FLIGHT PLAN

Your fully sharable Flight Plan! Cut this out and post it where it will matter the most! Get the people in your life involved with your Moonshot to help you achieve your personal growth goals, and to capitalize on your strengths whenever they need them!

Be sure to print legibly! When you are done, cut along the dotted line. It will fit inside a five-by-seven frame!

MY FLIGHT PLAN

NAME:

MY MOONSHOT:

YOU CAN RELY ON ME TO   Here are a few strengths or behaviors that you can rely on me to do consistently:

THINGS I NEED TO IMPROVE   Help me by watching for these things and letting me know when I am doing them [especially in real time]:

TOP FIVE STRENGTHS
1]   2]   3]   4]   5]

MY MOTIVATORS   These are the things that give me energy:

MY STRESSORS   These are the things that drain my energy:

SUPPORT CARDS

Based on your Flight Plan, use these cards to get support from the people around you. These can be passed out in meetings, given to team members to keep, or stuck on your refrigerator at home.

PLEASE SUPPORT ME

Watch out for me and let me know if I do this:

Take up all the air in a meeting.

This is the benefit I hope to gain:

To create space for others to share their opinions

before I weigh in.

PLEASE SUPPORT ME

Watch out for me and let me know if I do this:

This is the benefit I hope to gain:

PLEASE SUPPORT ME

Watch out for me and let me know if I do this:

This is the benefit I hope to gain:

PLEASE SUPPORT ME

Watch out for me and let me know if I do this:

This is the benefit I hope to gain:

PLEASE SUPPORT ME

Watch out for me and let me know if I do this:

This is the benefit I hope to gain:

PLEASE SUPPORT ME

Watch out for me and let me know if I do this:

This is the benefit I hope to gain:

PLEASE SUPPORT ME

Watch out for me and let me know if I do this:

This is the benefit I hope to gain:

PLEASE SUPPORT ME

Watch out for me and let me know if I do this:

This is the benefit I hope to gain:

FLIGHT PLAN
WORKSHEET EXAMPLES

Check out what other BIGGBY family members have found for themselves by working out their Flight Plan. Also consider the act of vulnerability on display here. They recognize that the more people they can bring in to look at their weaknesses and limitations, the more help they can get learning new ways to be. Take it from Richard Yurcak, 2017 BIGGBY COFFEE Barista of the Year: "Vulnerability is strength."

MY FLIGHT PLAN

THIRD SESSION 2019 | September—December

MY MOONSHOT:
I WANT TO LEAVE BEHIND A LEGACY OF LOVE AND ACCEPTANCE THROUGH OWNING A BIGGBY(S), BECOMING AN AUTHOR, HOLDING A POLITICA OFFICE AND STARTING A NON PROFIT

YOU CAN RELY ON ME TO Here are a few strengths or behaviors that you can rely on me to do consistently:
GIVE HONEST FEEDBACK
SUPPORT YOUR GROWTH
PROBLEM SOLVE

THINGS I NEED TO IMPROVE Help me by watching for these things and letting me know when I am doing them [especially in real time]:
NOT PLANNING ENOUGH
THINKING THROUGH DETAILS
ASKING FOR HELP

TOP FIVE STRENGTHS
1] RESTORATIVE   2] ACHIEVE   3] LEARNER   4] IDEATION   5] INDIVIDUALIST

MY MOTIVATORS These are the things that give me energy
SUCCESS
LARGE DIFFICULT PROJECTS
DATA TRENDS
RE ORG

MY STRESSORS These are the things that drain energy
COMMUNICATION

Rebecca Vacek, BIGGBY COFFEE Home Office

MY FLIGHT PLAN

FIRST SESSION 2019 | January—April

MY MOONSHOT:

To laugh at home every day and to die knowing that I've helped no fewer than one million people to build a life they love — one Moonshot at a time.

YOU CAN RELY ON ME TO Here are a few strengths or behaviors that you can rely on me to do consistently:

- Care about people, with genuine interest, and provide support.
- Analyze - data, situations, problems - deeply & from multiple perspectives.
- Give full effort to what I'm doing - to get the job done.

THINGS I NEED TO IMPROVE Help me by watching for these things and letting me know when I am doing them [especially in real time]:

- Condescending tone
- Listening to respond
- Saying "no" to things - particularly things that don't make use of my talents.

TOP FIVE STRENGTHS

1] Strategic	2] Achiever	3] Competition	4] Analytical	5] Activator
		* Empathy *	* Developer *	* Futuristic *

MY MOTIVATORS These are the things that give me energy

- Making a positive difference for people, especially when my advice proves useful.
- Being complimented on a job well done
- Listening to people's concerns & needs
- Encouraging others to do their best.
- Creating things - systems & tools
- Seeing things I create get used.
- Experimenting

MY STRESSORS These are the things that drain energy

- Saying no
- Working in a tense environment
- Making "big" decisions independently.
- Disorganization / clutter
- Staying engaged in a conversation when there's time pressure.

Jeremy DeRuiter, BIGGBY COFFEE Home Office

RECOMMENDED READING

"I do believe that the act of learning is a way to keep yourself growing, and in many ways I think if we all just simply agreed to repeat the cycle of 'learn—grow—share' forever, our communities would be in a constant state of improvement." —*Bob Fish*

Reading and sharing books with the people in your life gets everyone engaged with the same ideas and helps create a shared language. That kind of alignment can get you powerful results, faster. Here's a partial list of books we believe are powerful tools for personal and organizational growth. Now that you have written your Flight Plan, dive into something that will help YOU grow!

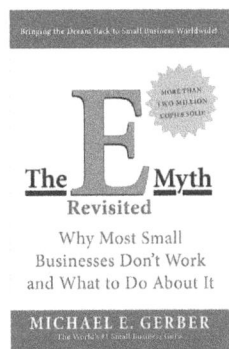

We provide a copy of this book to new Owner/Operators when they sign their first franchise agreement with us. It provides powerful ideas for growing a business, including understanding what you're looking to accomplish in your life through your business—your Primary Aim. This book is part of the DNA of *The Moonshot Guidebook*.

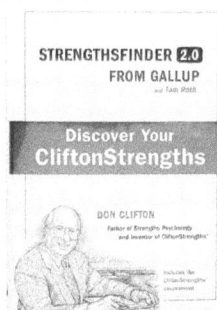

The central premise of the book is to worry less about fixing your weaknesses and more about how to use your strengths as a catapult to success. People often say after taking the Clifton StrengthsFinder test, "Yep, they got me." Having a test tell you what you might already know has a clarifying effect that is empowering.

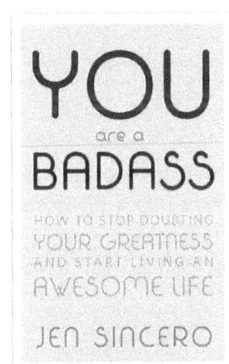

The Moonshot Guidebook will help you create a blueprint for building a life you love, and *You Are a Badass* will give you the motivation to get started today! Jen helps you look in the mirror to figure out how you're getting in your own way while teaching you to love yourself!

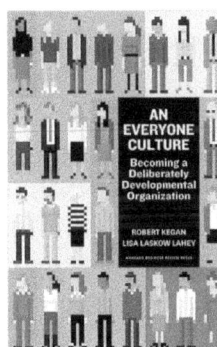

A look inside three DDOs—deliberately developmental organizations. They have baked personal growth into the way they operate their businesses. The Flight Plan is an adaptation from the Baseball Card practice at Bridgewater. Check out chapter 6 for the powerful Immunity to Change activity.

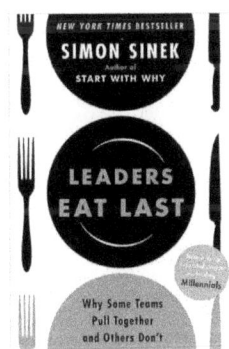

Every leader should read this book. Its picture of servant leadership and creating a circle of safety is a powerful demonstration of how to be at work and in life. Check out chapter 6 for a great explanation about the power of writing down goals and using visual details. Super Moonshot-y.

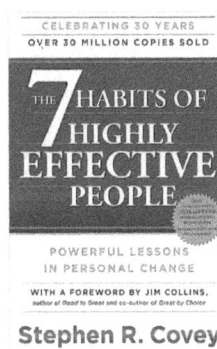

Covey's seven habits cover a tremendous amount of ground for going to work on yourself. The second habit, "Begin with the end in mind," starts with visualizing your own funeral, then has you develop a personal mission statement of who and how you want to be, and then encourages you to reflect on what you've made the center of your life.

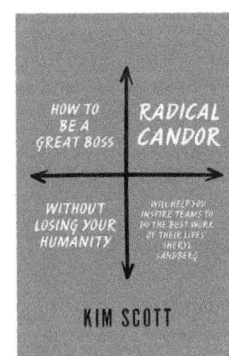

This book's target audience is managers, but the lessons on how to give direct guidance to a person, while also demonstrating that you care for them, is advice that anyone can use. And if you ARE a manager, buy this book right now. There is a ton of practical advice on how to be a better boss and get better results.

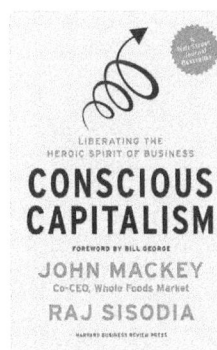

This is the book that the leaders of BIGGBY COFFEE read in 2015 that set us on our path to find our Higher Purpose. It's a detailed argument for (and guide to) running a company for more than just profit. Check out chapter 14 for practices to develop your emotional, systems, and physical intelligence.

CLIMBING TO THE STARS

Dreaming is a delightful experience. As children, we dreamt all the time. Life was our oyster; we could do anything; we were full of big dreams, and it was invigorating and inspiring to think about what could be.

But then the real world comes up and smacks us in the face. Most of us have been told in one way or another to put our dreams aside. Dreams are silly, and now we have to be an adult. We are caught up in being sensible, getting our work done, paying the bills, doing the laundry, keeping the house tidy, feeding the dog. Fantastic romantic lives are for the people on TV. We are okay with watching them live their lives, being voyeurs of their success. But it can't be us.

Why?

We don't know where we are going, and we don't have a plan in place to get us to this destination. We hope you have immersed yourself in the process of dreaming BIGG earlier in this workbook, reaching for the stars in the previous few exercises. We hope you felt that butterfly in your belly when you wrote your Moonshot. We hope this process has got you excited.

Now we have to engage a process for building a plan that will help you set that butterfly free so you can see a life you love starting to emerge right in front of your eyes.

We must now implement and execute. We have to break your Moonshot down into manageable increments.

If you write a list of all the things you need to do to accomplish your Moonshot today, it would seem and feel overwhelming. The following sheet has been developed to break it down into incremental steps that will get you to the finish line, having built something special that will have led you to a life that you love. You are building the rocket ship that will land you in your rocking chair, having accomplished your Moonshot.

This process takes time and practice. The first few times you go through it, don't worry about getting it right; just make sure to get it done. Things will come more and more into focus as sessions and years go by. It is important to make sure to keep working on this process and improving it. You will be amazed at the results. What once seemed unattainable will soon seem easy, and your next set of goals will feel like a stretch . . . and then you will meet those goals. The momentum will build, and at some point in the not-too-distant future, you will look around and be amazed at what you have accomplished.

We hope you engage, and we hope you take it seriously and therefore take your life seriously. We all have one opportunity to build a life we love—so let's make the best of it. Let's be an example for everyday people—people who live next door—by being exceptional and by doing extraordinary things!

How much money will I need to do the things I wish to do? By when will I need that money?

I will need this much

$ _____

by this date to reach my goals

_____ / _____ / _____

TAKE INVENTORY

An important piece of laying out your path to your Moonshot is to make sure you will have what it takes to get there. Look through the work you've done so far to determine how much money you will need in order to arrive at your Moonshot. Pay attention to the things you will need to purchase, the places you want to visit, and the style of life you want to live through your retirement. Online tools/apps like Mint (www.mint.com) and NerdWallet (www.nerdwallet.com) have a ton of resources for financial planning and budgeting that you can use to help set these goals and work toward them!

CLIMBING TO THE STARS | SESSION ONE

Here's where things get exciting. It's time to start laying out the plan for exactly how you will accomplish your Moonshot. You're going to be filling this out from the top to the bottom, setting goals that will lead you to accomplishing the previous step. You might also want to refer back to your two-, ten-, and twenty-year visions in the Moonshot Worksheet.

MY MOONSHOT   Write its current iteration here:

_____

_____

_____

_____

_____

FIVE-YEAR GOALS   Date five years from now: _____

What two things do you need to accomplish within five years to feel comfortable you will accomplish your Moonshot?:

_____

_____

_____

_____

_____

ONE-YEAR GOALS   Date one year from now: _____

What three goals do you need to accomplish within one year to feel comfortable you will accomplish your five-year goals?:

_____

_____

_____

_____

_____

SESSION GOALS   Date four months from now: _____

What three things are you going to do this session to ensure you meet your one-year goals?:

_____

_____

_____

_____

_____

Once you have completed this sheet, go to your calendar and add the target dates for your goals and also assign dates to accomplish the other details from your two-year vision.

Don't forget to . . . *FUEL UP*. Share your plan with the people in your life who will help you get there!

READY TO LAUNCH

Congratulations! You are ready for launch! Where you stand right this moment in time is unique. You will never be the you that you are right at this moment. Write about what you feel about what you have written and learned so far. Tell your future self what you plan to accomplish by the end of the year. You will be prompted to return to this letter at the end of the year to read what you wrote and measure against it.

T-MINUS 10 . . .

It's time. You have done a ton of preparation to get you to this moment. You took a deep look into your future to determine who, where, and what you want to be in two, ten, and twenty years. You boiled that down into a personally powerful Moonshot Statement and wrote a visually descriptive Lunar Landscape. You took a look in the mirror to develop your Flight Plan so you will be the person you need to be in order to reach your Moonshot. And you crafted your plan to Climb to the Stars so you know the big steps you need to take to steadily progress toward achieving your dreams. Now it's time to live into that future—week in and week out.

What follows are Mission Sheets for every week of the year.

You will start by setting your areas of focus. These are the places in your life where pouring your focus into them from one week to another will power you toward reaching your short- and long-term goals. Your ares of focus likely won't change each week. For example, if your goal is to complete a marathon, your focus might be on diet, exercise, and adding distance.

In addition to the three areas of focus, you will also set a focus built specifically off of your Flight Plan. It could be a specific way of capitalizing on one of your strengths, or a way to work on one of the areas you identified you need to improve on, or to make a plan to engage in things that keep you motivated.

Targets are the things you need to accomplish over the next week to advance in each area of focus. Using the previous example, your targets for adding distance might include a) eight-mile run Tuesday, b) five-mile run on Thursday, c) twelve-mile run on Saturday. They are concrete tasks that you can accomplish.

Your areas of focus and targets are not meant to encompass all of the tasks you have to complete over the course of a week.

These are the specific things that will help you advance toward accomplishing your Moonshot. Use the Notes section (page 108) to keep track of the other tasks that keep the machine of your life and work moving fluidly forward.

WEEKLY MISSION SHEETS   / /   to   / /

1] _____

2] _____

3] _____

WEEK 1

FOCUS 1 _____

Target a _____

Target b _____

Target c _____

FOCUS 2 _____

Target a _____

Target b _____

Target c _____

FOCUS 3 _____

Target a _____

Target b _____

Target c _____

FLIGHT PLAN FOCUS _____

Target a _____

Target b _____

Target c _____

WEEK 2

FOCUS 1 _____

Target a _____

Target b _____

Target c _____

FOCUS 2 _____

Target a _____

Target b _____

Target c _____

FOCUS 3 _____

Target a _____

Target b _____

Target c _____

FLIGHT PLAN FOCUS _____

Target a _____

Target b _____

Target c _____

WEEKLY MISSION SHEETS   /   /   to   /   /

WEEK 3

FOCUS 1 _____

Target a _____

Target b _____

Target c _____

FOCUS 2 _____

Target a _____

Target b _____

Target c _____

FOCUS 3 _____

Target a _____

Target b _____

Target c _____

FLIGHT PLAN FOCUS _____

_____

Target a _____

Target b _____

Target c _____

WEEK 4

FOCUS 1 _____

Target a _____

Target b _____

Target c _____

FOCUS 2 _____

Target a _____

Target b _____

Target c _____

FOCUS 3 _____

Target a _____

Target b _____

Target c _____

FLIGHT PLAN FOCUS _____

_____

Target a _____

Target b _____

Target c _____

NOTES Did you hit all of your targets last week? If not, diagnose it below and plan accordingly for this week!

Week 1] _____

Week 2] _____

Week 3] _____

Week 4] _____

WEEKLY MISSION SHEETS

SESSION ONE GOALS

Put the same goals that you wrote in Climbing to the Stars here.

1] _____

2] _____

3] _____

WEEK 5

FOCUS 1 _____

Target a _____

Target b _____

Target c _____

FOCUS 2 _____

Target a _____

Target b _____

Target c _____

FOCUS 3 _____

Target a _____

Target b _____

Target c _____

FLIGHT PLAN FOCUS _____

_____

Target a _____

Target b _____

Target c _____

WEEK 6

FOCUS 1 _____

Target a _____

Target b _____

Target c _____

FOCUS 2 _____

Target a _____

Target b _____

Target c _____

FOCUS 3 _____

Target a _____

Target b _____

Target c _____

FLIGHT PLAN FOCUS _____

_____

Target a _____

Target b _____

Target c _____

WEEKLY MISSION SHEETS   /   /   to   /   /

WEEK 7

FOCUS 1 _____

Target a _____

Target b _____

Target c _____

FOCUS 2 _____

Target a _____

Target b _____

Target c _____

FOCUS 3 _____

Target a _____

Target b _____

Target c _____

FLIGHT PLAN FOCUS _____

_____

Target a _____

Target b _____

Target c _____

WEEK 8

FOCUS 1 _____

Target a _____

Target b _____

Target c _____

FOCUS 2 _____

Target a _____

Target b _____

Target c _____

FOCUS 3 _____

Target a _____

Target b _____

Target c _____

FLIGHT PLAN FOCUS _____

_____

Target a _____

Target b _____

Target c _____

NOTES Did you hit all of your targets last week? If not, diagnose it below and plan accordingly for this week!

Week 5] _____

Week 6] _____

Week 7] _____

Week 8] _____

WEEKLY MISSION SHEETS   /   /   to   /   /

1] _____

2] _____

3] _____

WEEK 9

FOCUS 1 _____

Target a _____

Target b _____

Target c _____

FOCUS 2 _____

Target a _____

Target b _____

Target c _____

FOCUS 3 _____

Target a _____

Target b _____

Target c _____

FLIGHT PLAN FOCUS _____

Target a _____

Target b _____

Target c _____

WEEK 10

FOCUS 1 _____

Target a _____

Target b _____

Target c _____

FOCUS 2 _____

Target a _____

Target b _____

Target c _____

FOCUS 3 _____

Target a _____

Target b _____

Target c _____

FLIGHT PLAN FOCUS _____

Target a _____

Target b _____

Target c _____

WEEKLY MISSION SHEETS   / /   to   / /

WEEK 11

FOCUS 1 _____

Target a _____

Target b _____

Target c _____

FOCUS 2 _____

Target a _____

Target b _____

Target c _____

FOCUS 3 _____

Target a _____

Target b _____

Target c _____

FLIGHT PLAN FOCUS _____

_____

Target a _____

Target b _____

Target c _____

WEEK 12

FOCUS 1 _____

Target a _____

Target b _____

Target c _____

FOCUS 2 _____

Target a _____

Target b _____

Target c _____

FOCUS 3 _____

Target a _____

Target b _____

Target c _____

FLIGHT PLAN FOCUS _____

_____

Target a _____

Target b _____

Target c _____

NOTES Did you hit all of your targets last week? If not, diagnose it below and plan accordingly for this week!

Week 9] _____

Week 10] _____

Week 11] _____

Week 12] _____

_____

WEEKLY MISSION SHEETS

/ / to / /

SESSION ONE GOALS

Put the same goals that you wrote in Climbing to the Stars here.

1] _____

2] _____

3] _____

WEEK 13

FOCUS 1 _____

Target a _____

Target b _____

Target c _____

FOCUS 2 _____

Target a _____

Target b _____

Target c _____

FOCUS 3 _____

Target a _____

Target b _____

Target c _____

FLIGHT PLAN FOCUS _____

_____

Target a _____

Target b _____

Target c _____

WEEK 14

FOCUS 1 _____

Target a _____

Target b _____

Target c _____

FOCUS 2 _____

Target a _____

Target b _____

Target c _____

FOCUS 3 _____

Target a _____

Target b _____

Target c _____

FLIGHT PLAN FOCUS _____

_____

Target a _____

Target b _____

Target c _____

WEEKLY MISSION SHEETS   / /   to   / /

WEEK 15

FOCUS 1 _____

Target a _____

Target b _____

Target c _____

FOCUS 2 _____

Target a _____

Target b _____

Target c _____

FOCUS 3 _____

Target a _____

Target b _____

Target c _____

FLIGHT PLAN FOCUS _____

_____

Target a _____

Target b _____

Target c _____

WEEK 16

FOCUS 1 _____

Target a _____

Target b _____

Target c _____

FOCUS 2 _____

Target a _____

Target b _____

Target c _____

FOCUS 3 _____

Target a _____

Target b _____

Target c _____

FLIGHT PLAN FOCUS _____

_____

Target a _____

Target b _____

Target c _____

NOTES Did you hit all of your targets last week? If not, diagnose it below and plan accordingly for this week!

Week 13] _____

Week 14] _____

Week 15] _____

Week 16] _____

_____

WEEKLY MISSION SHEETS / / to / /

WEEK 17

FOCUS 1 _____

Target a _____
Target b _____
Target c _____

FOCUS 3 _____

Target a _____
Target b _____
Target c _____

FOCUS 2 _____

Target a _____
Target b _____
Target c _____

FLIGHT PLAN FOCUS _____

Target a _____
Target b _____
Target c _____

NOTES Did you hit all of your targets last week? If not, diagnose it below and plan accordingly for this week!

Week 17] _____

CONGRATULATIONS,
VISIONAUT

SESSION ONE
COMPLETE

ROCKETS DON'T HAVE REARVIEW MIRRORS

Perhaps that's why we aren't prone to looking behind us to see what we've accomplished. This is your moment to pause and take stock of how the previous four months have gone before you dive into the work of Session Two.

Did I accomplish each of my Session Goals? If not, why not?

_____

_____

_____

Look at what you just wrote down. Have you taken responsibility for your own actions or inaction? If you find that you are the object of a sentence rather than the subject, that could be a good sign. For example, "I got passed over for promotion." In that sentence, you're not doing anything. Someone else did the passing over. If you fell short of achieving your goals, take full accountability by stating exactly what you did or failed to do. This is a crucial step in building your integrity and accomplishing future goals. Phew. Radical candor, right?

What could I have done differently over the last four months to get even better results than I did? Did I miss any opportunities?

_____

_____

_____

What are all the things, specifically, that I have achieved in my life over the last four months (including non-Moonshot pursuits)?

_____

_____

_____

Look back at your Session One Flight Plan. How have I taken advantage of my strengths? How have I improved myself?

_____

_____

_____

MOONSHOT WORKSHEET | SESSION TWO

Welcome to Session Two! You've had four months to work on creating your Moonshot—on paper and in your life. Visioning is an iterative process: you start wherever and however, just to get going. Then you let some time pass, live some life, and then return to working on your vision. Your perspective and circumstances change over time, and the dreams for your life will come to you with greater clarity and inspiration each time.

This session begins with a mix of new questions and some that you answered in Session One. We encourage you to start fresh on those repeating questions—don't look back at what you wrote first or copy it in here. You might uncover some new things for yourself using this method. Then, once you're done, you'll have a chance to compare, contrast, and see if any differences tell you something new about yourself and your future.

Happy visioning!

1) What song lyric, famous quote, poetry verse, or saying do I find inspirational? Why?

2) How do I center myself? How do I recharge?

3) What is one of my favorite memories of time spent with a loved one?

4) When I am at my very best, how do I treat the people in my life?

_____

_____

_____

_____

_____

_____

5) Who are the people most important to my life today?

_____

_____

_____

_____

_____

_____

6) Who will be most important to my future? This can include people you haven't even met yet—you can cast a vision for them too! Just describe them in detail. When will you need to meet them? How will you meet them?

_____

_____

_____

_____

_____

_____

7) Two years from today, how would I like to be spending my time?

The date two years from today: _____   My age, two years from today: _____

_____

_____

_____

_____

_____

_____

8) What about in ten years?   The date ten years from today: _____   My age, ten years from today: _____

_____

_____

_____

_____

_____

9) And twenty years from now?   The date twenty years from today: _____   My age, twenty years from today: _____

_____

_____

_____

_____

_____

_____

10) Okay, now compare what you have written here to what you wrote in Session One. Did anything change? What stands out?

_____

_____

_____

_____

_____

_____

11) Boil down your answers to the previous questions to one or, at most, three words per question.

1] _____   2] _____   3] _____

4] _____   5] _____   6] _____

7] _____   8] _____   9] _____

10] _____

12) Do you see a theme in your answers? What does this tell you?

_____

_____

_____

_____

_____

_____

MY MOONSHOT

Reflect on what you have written in the Moonshot Worksheets and boil it down to a simple statement that sums it up for you.

If you could accomplish one thing in your life, what would it be?

_____

_____

_____

_____

_____

DESCRIBE YOUR LUNAR LANDSCAPE

Imagine that someone has time travelled into your future and spends time documenting your life once you've accomplished your Moonshot. Describe in vivid detail ten pictures that the time traveler will take of your future life.

1] _____

2] _____

3] _____

4] _____

5] _____

6] _____

7] _____

8] _____

9] _____

10] _____

We would LOVE to see your Moonshot! Take a picture of this page after you have completed your answers and send it in to moonshot@biggby.com.

FLIGHT PLAN WORKSHEET | SESSION TWO

It is time to return to the Flight Plan you developed in Session One to see if updates are necessary. The work you have done on yourself over the last four months and any new feedback you have received from the people in your life in the meantime could mean that you should have a new area of focus for Session Two.

1) Give your guidebook to five other people to answer the question: What can you rely on me for?

1]

2]

3]

4]

5]

2) Now, using your Top Five as a starting point, write out what you wish your Top Ten would look like (including making changes to your Top Five. See page 107 for the full list of strengths):

1]   2]   3]   4]   5]

6]   7]   8]   9]   10]

3) Where in my life am I being inauthentic? Are there places or people with whom I am not being the most true version of myself?

4) Based on the previous answer, what changes can I make in the way I act to walk my talk and show up fully as myself?

5) If my boss or partner were to give me one piece of advice, what would it be?

6) What have my boss or partner and I talked about in the recent past that I need additional work on?

7) If my closest, most critical friend were to give me one piece of advice, what would it be?

_____

_____

_____

_____

8) Do any recent critiques suggest a theme of something that I should be trying to improve? If yes, write that here:

_____

_____

_____

_____

9) Which parts of my work style or the way I communicate cause the most trouble? How do I frustrate people?

_____

_____

_____

_____

10) Motivators – What in my life or work environment motivates and excites me?

_____

_____

_____

_____

11) Stressors – What are the things that stress me out or take a lot of energy from me?

_____

_____

_____

_____

Congratulations! You have almost completed this step in the process! All that is left is to transcribe the information on this worksheet to your Flight Plan on the next page and then carry that information with you and use it to communicate with the people in your life for the coming session.

Don't forget to . . . _FUEL UP._ Share your plan with the people in your life who will help you get there!

MY FLIGHT PLAN

SECOND SESSION | May–August

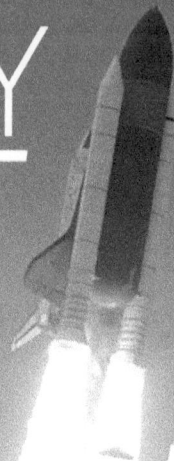

MY MOONSHOT:

_____

_____

_____

YOU CAN RELY ON ME TO   Here are a few strengths or behaviors that you can rely on me to do consistently:

_____

_____

_____

THINGS I NEED TO IMPROVE   Help me by watching for these things and letting me know when I am doing them [especially in real time]:

_____

_____

_____

TOP FIVE STRENGTHS

1] _____ 2] _____ 3] _____ 4] _____ 5] _____

MY MOTIVATORS   These are the things that give me energy:

_____

_____

_____

_____

_____

_____

_____

_____

MY STRESSORS   These are the things that drain my energy:

_____

_____

_____

_____

_____

_____

_____

_____

SHARABLE FLIGHT PLAN

Your fully sharable Flight Plan! Cut this out and post it where it will matter the most! Get the people in your life involved with your Moonshot to help you achieve your personal growth goals, and to capitalize on your strengths whenever they need them!

Be sure to print legibly! When you are done, cut along the dotted line. It will fit inside a five-by-seven frame!

MY
FLIGHT
PLAN

NAME:

MY MOONSHOT:

YOU CAN RELY ON ME TO   Here are a few strengths or behaviors that you can rely on me to do consistently:

THINGS I NEED TO IMPROVE   Help me by watching for these things and letting me know when I am doing them [especially in real time]:

TOP FIVE STRENGTHS
1]   2]   3]   4]   5]

MY MOTIVATORS   These are the things that give me energy: MY STRESSORS   These are the things that drain my energy:

SUPPORT CARDS

Based on your Flight Plan, use these cards to get support from the people around you. These can be passed out in meetings, given to team members to keep, or stuck on your refrigerator at home.

PLEASE SUPPORT ME
Watch out for me and let me know if I do this:

_____

This is the benefit I hope to gain:

_____

PLEASE SUPPORT ME
Watch out for me and let me know if I do this:

_____

This is the benefit I hope to gain:

_____

PLEASE SUPPORT ME
Watch out for me and let me know if I do this:

_____

This is the benefit I hope to gain:

_____

PLEASE SUPPORT ME
Watch out for me and let me know if I do this:

_____

This is the benefit I hope to gain:

_____

PLEASE SUPPORT ME
Watch out for me and let me know if I do this:

_____

This is the benefit I hope to gain:

_____

PLEASE SUPPORT ME
Watch out for me and let me know if I do this:

_____

This is the benefit I hope to gain:

_____

PLEASE SUPPORT ME
Watch out for me and let me know if I do this:

_____

This is the benefit I hope to gain:

_____

PLEASE SUPPORT ME
Watch out for me and let me know if I do this:

_____

This is the benefit I hope to gain:

_____

CLIMBING TO THE STARS | SESSION TWO

You've been here before. It's time to start laying out the plan for exactly how you will accomplish your Moonshot. You're going to be filling this out from the top to the bottom, setting goals that will lead you to accomplishing the previous step. You might also want to refer back to your two-, ten-, and twenty-year visions in the Moonshot Worksheet.

MY MOONSHOT   Write its current iteration here:

_____

_____

_____

_____

FIVE-YEAR GOALS   Date five years from now: _____

What two things do you need to accomplish within five years to feel comfortable you will accomplish your Moonshot?:

_____

_____

_____

_____

ONE-YEAR GOALS   Date one year from now: _____

What three goals do you need to accomplish within one year to feel comfortable you will accomplish your five-year goals?:

_____

_____

_____

_____

SESSION GOALS   Date four months from now: _____

What three things are you going to do this session to ensure you meet your one-year goals?:

_____

_____

_____

_____

_____

Once you have completed this sheet, go to your calendar and add the target dates for your goals and also assign dates to accomplish the other details from your two-year vision.

Don't forget to . . . *FUEL UP.* Share your plan with the people in your life who will help you get there!

WEEKLY MISSION SHEETS   / /   to   / /

SESSION TWO GOALS

Put the same goals that you wrote in Climbing to the Stars here.

1] _____

2] _____

3] _____

WEEK 18

FOCUS 1 _____

Target a _____

Target b _____

Target c _____

FOCUS 2 _____

Target a _____

Target b _____

Target c _____

FOCUS 3 _____

Target a _____

Target b _____

Target c _____

FLIGHT PLAN FOCUS _____

_____

Target a _____

Target b _____

Target c _____

WEEK 19

FOCUS 1 _____

Target a _____

Target b _____

Target c _____

FOCUS 2 _____

Target a _____

Target b _____

Target c _____

FOCUS 3 _____

Target a _____

Target b _____

Target c _____

FLIGHT PLAN FOCUS _____

_____

Target a _____

Target b _____

Target c _____

WEEKLY MISSION SHEETS   / /   to   / /

WEEK 20

FOCUS 1 _____

Target a _____

Target b _____

Target c _____

FOCUS 2 _____

Target a _____

Target b _____

Target c _____

FOCUS 3 _____

Target a _____

Target b _____

Target c _____

FLIGHT PLAN FOCUS _____

Target a _____

Target b _____

Target c _____

WEEK 21

FOCUS 1 _____

Target a _____

Target b _____

Target c _____

FOCUS 2 _____

Target a _____

Target b _____

Target c _____

FOCUS 3 _____

Target a _____

Target b _____

Target c _____

FLIGHT PLAN FOCUS _____

Target a _____

Target b _____

Target c _____

NOTES Did you hit all of your targets last week? If not, diagnose it below and plan accordingly for this week!

Week 18] _____

Week 19] _____

Week 20] _____

Week 21] _____

WEEKLY MISSION SHEETS   / /   to   / /

1] _____

2] _____

3] _____

WEEK 22

FOCUS 1 _____

Target a _____

Target b _____

Target c _____

FOCUS 2 _____

Target a _____

Target b _____

Target c _____

FOCUS 3 _____

Target a _____

Target b _____

Target c _____

FLIGHT PLAN FOCUS _____

_____

Target a _____

Target b _____

Target c _____

WEEK 23

FOCUS 1 _____

Target a _____

Target b _____

Target c _____

FOCUS 2 _____

Target a _____

Target b _____

Target c _____

FOCUS 3 _____

Target a _____

Target b _____

Target c _____

FLIGHT PLAN FOCUS _____

_____

Target a _____

Target b _____

Target c _____

WEEKLY MISSION SHEETS   / / to / /

WEEK 24

FOCUS 1 _____

Target a _____
Target b _____
Target c _____

FOCUS 2 _____

Target a _____
Target b _____
Target c _____

FOCUS 3 _____

Target a _____
Target b _____
Target c _____

FLIGHT PLAN FOCUS _____

_____

Target a _____
Target b _____
Target c _____

WEEK 25

FOCUS 1 _____

Target a _____
Target b _____
Target c _____

FOCUS 2 _____

Target a _____
Target b _____
Target c _____

FOCUS 3 _____

Target a _____
Target b _____
Target c _____

FLIGHT PLAN FOCUS _____

_____

Target a _____
Target b _____
Target c _____

NOTES Did you hit all of your targets last week? If not, diagnose it below and plan accordingly for this week!

Week 22] _____

Week 23] _____

Week 24] _____

Week 25] _____

WEEKLY MISSION SHEETS

/ / to / /

SESSION TWO GOALS

Put the same goals that you wrote in Climbing to the Stars here.

1] _____

2] _____

3] _____

WEEK 26

FOCUS 1 _____

Target a _____

Target b _____

Target c _____

FOCUS 2 _____

Target a _____

Target b _____

Target c _____

FOCUS 3 _____

Target a _____

Target b _____

Target c _____

FLIGHT PLAN FOCUS _____

Target a _____

Target b _____

Target c _____

WEEK 27

FOCUS 1 _____

Target a _____

Target b _____

Target c _____

FOCUS 2 _____

Target a _____

Target b _____

Target c _____

FOCUS 3 _____

Target a _____

Target b _____

Target c _____

FLIGHT PLAN FOCUS _____

Target a _____

Target b _____

Target c _____

WEEKLY MISSION SHEETS   /   /   to   /   /

WEEK 28

FOCUS 1 _____

Target a _____

Target b _____

Target c _____

FOCUS 2 _____

Target a _____

Target b _____

Target c _____

FOCUS 3 _____

Target a _____

Target b _____

Target c _____

FLIGHT PLAN FOCUS _____

_____

Target a _____

Target b _____

Target c _____

WEEK 29

FOCUS 1 _____

Target a _____

Target b _____

Target c _____

FOCUS 2 _____

Target a _____

Target b _____

Target c _____

FOCUS 3 _____

Target a _____

Target b _____

Target c _____

FLIGHT PLAN FOCUS _____

_____

Target a _____

Target b _____

Target c _____

NOTES Did you hit all of your targets last week? If not, diagnose it below and plan accordingly for this week!

Week 26] _____

Week 27] _____

Week 28] _____

Week 29] _____

WEEKLY MISSION SHEETS   / / to / /

SESSION TWO GOALS

Put the same goals that you wrote in Climbing to the Stars here.

1] _____

2] _____

3] _____

WEEK 30

FOCUS 1 _____	
Target a _____	
Target b _____	
Target c _____	
FOCUS 2 _____	
Target a _____	
Target b _____	
Target c _____	
FOCUS 3 _____	
Target a _____	
Target b _____	
Target c _____	
FLIGHT PLAN FOCUS _____	
Target a _____	
Target b _____	
Target c _____	

WEEK 31

FOCUS 1 _____	
Target a _____	
Target b _____	
Target c _____	
FOCUS 2 _____	
Target a _____	
Target b _____	
Target c _____	
FOCUS 3 _____	
Target a _____	
Target b _____	
Target c _____	
FLIGHT PLAN FOCUS _____	
Target a _____	
Target b _____	
Target c _____	

WEEKLY MISSION SHEETS   /   /   to   /   /

WEEK 32

FOCUS 1 _____

Target a _____

Target b _____

Target c _____

FOCUS 2 _____

Target a _____

Target b _____

Target c _____

FOCUS 3 _____

Target a _____

Target b _____

Target c _____

FLIGHT PLAN FOCUS _____

Target a _____

Target b _____

Target c _____

WEEK 33

FOCUS 1 _____

Target a _____

Target b _____

Target c _____

FOCUS 2 _____

Target a _____

Target b _____

Target c _____

FOCUS 3 _____

Target a _____

Target b _____

Target c _____

FLIGHT PLAN FOCUS _____

Target a _____

Target b _____

Target c _____

NOTES Did you hit all of your targets last week? If not, diagnose it below and plan accordingly for this week!

Week 30] _____

Week 31] _____

Week 32] _____

Week 33] _____

WEEKLY MISSION SHEETS

/ / to / /

WEEK 34

FOCUS 1 _____

Target a _____

Target b _____

Target c _____

FOCUS 2 _____

Target a _____

Target b _____

Target c _____

FOCUS 3 _____

Target a _____

Target b _____

Target c _____

FLIGHT PLAN FOCUS _____

Target a _____

Target b _____

Target c _____

NOTES Did you hit all of your targets last week? If not, diagnose it below and plan accordingly for this week!

Week 34] _____

CONGRATULATIONS,
VISIONAUT

SESSION TWO
COMPLETE

PULL
INTO THE DOCK,
VISIONAUT

You are more than halfway through this year's voyage. This is your moment to stop and take inventory of how your journey has gone before launching into Session Three.

Did I accomplish each of my Session Goals? If not, why not?

_____

_____

_____

Look at what you just wrote down. Have you taken responsibility for your own actions or inaction? Refer back to the directions for this on page 57.

What could I have done differently over the last four months to get even better results than I did? Did I miss any opportunities?

_____

_____

_____

What are all the things, specifically, that I have achieved in my life over the last four months (including non-Moonshot pursuits)?

_____

_____

_____

Look back at your Session Two Flight Plan. How have I taken advantage of my strengths? How have I improved myself?

_____

_____

_____

Before you go! Please send along any suggestions you have accumulated in the back of the book, or any other questions or comments you have about *The Moonshot Guidebook* to moonshot@biggby.com.

MOONSHOT WORKSHEET | SESSION THREE

Welcome to Session THREE! You're heading into the home stretch of the year. In the world of BIGGBY, this is the busiest, most exciting time of the year for us. We just hosted our annual BIGGBY Nation Summit in August, pulling together hundreds and hundreds of the BIGGBY family to celebrate the accomplishments of the past year and to look forward to everything that the new year will bring for us. Let's make Session Three the same for you too.

Once again, Visionaut, you will begin this session with a mix of new questions and some that you answered in previous sessions. Every session and every year, look at these questions with the eyes of the current you—don't go back to what you wrote and copy it in. That will keep your vision frozen in time from when you first wrote it. This isn't time travel; it's a voyage to your Moonshot!

Happy visioning!

1) What does a perfect day of work look like?

_____

_____

_____

_____

2) What does a perfect day of work feel like?

_____

_____

_____

_____

3) What will be the best vacation I ever take?

_____

_____

_____

_____

4) What is the most valuable way I can spend my time?

_____

_____

_____

_____

5) What principles or values do I want my life to be built upon? Use the activity on the following page for help!

_____

_____

_____

_____

Begin by choosing the fifteen things you value most. Then, from those, select just five. Finally, narrow it down to the two things that you value most in life.

First: Choose Fifteen	Second: Choose Five	Third: Choose Two
Flexibility	Flexibility	Flexibility
Generosity	Generosity	Generosity
Courage	Courage	Courage
Dedication	Dedication	Dedication
Positivity	Positivity	Positivity
Enthusiasm	Enthusiasm	Enthusiasm
Authenticity	Authenticity	Authenticity
Mindfulness	Mindfulness	Mindfulness
Fitness	Fitness	Fitness
Creativity	Creativity	Creativity
Individuality	Individuality	Individuality
Adventure	Adventure	Adventure
Diversity	Diversity	Diversity
Peace	Peace	Peace
Empowerment	Empowerment	Empowerment
Spirituality	Spirituality	Spirituality
Follow-through	Follow-through	Follow-through
Cooperation	Cooperation	Cooperation
Desire	Desire	Desire
Knowledge	Knowledge	Knowledge
Freedom	Freedom	Freedom
Loyalty	Loyalty	Loyalty
Achievement	Achievement	Achievement
Gratitude	Gratitude	Gratitude
Appreciation	Appreciation	Appreciation
Family	Family	Family
Challenge	Challenge	Challenge
Trust	Trust	Trust
Romance	Romance	Romance
Dependability	Dependability	Dependability
Respect	Respect	Respect
Curiosity	Curiosity	Curiosity
Fun	Fun	Fun
Organization	Organization	Organization
Stability	Stability	Stability
Confidence	Confidence	Confidence
Wisdom	Wisdom	Wisdom
Legacy	Legacy	Legacy
Beauty	Beauty	Beauty
Community	Community	Community

This activity is inspired by a values activity the Dale Carnegie Institute offers—seek them out!

6) What does it mean to me to be healthy and thriving in each of these areas of life?

Family: _____

Friends: _____

Work: _____

My body: _____

My mind: _____

My inner spirit: _____

7) Two years from today, how would I like to be spending my time?

The date two years from today: _____   My age, two years from today: _____

_____

_____

_____

_____

_____

_____

8) What about in ten years?   The date ten years from today: _____   My age, ten years from today: _____

_____

_____

_____

_____

_____

_____

9) And twenty years from now?   The date twenty years from today: _____   My age, twenty years from today: _____

_____

_____

_____

_____

_____

10) Okay, now compare what you have written here to what you wrote in Session Two. Did anything change? What stands out?

_____

_____

_____

_____

_____

_____

_____

MY MOONSHOT

Reflect on what you have written in the Moonshot Worksheet and boil it down to a simple statement that sums it up for you.

If you could accomplish one thing in your life, what would it be?

_____

_____

_____

DESCRIBE YOUR LUNAR LANDSCAPE

Write out what your life looks like, having reached your Moonshot. Describe a day in your life, from beginning to end. Where are you? Who is with you? How do you spend your time? What do you think and feel when you wake up and as you fall asleep?

_____

_____

_____

_____

_____

_____

_____

_____

_____

_____

_____

_____

_____

_____

_____

_____

_____

We would LOVE to see your Moonshot! Take a picture of this page after you have completed your answers and send it in to moonshot@biggby.com.

FLIGHT PLAN WORKSHEET | SESSION THREE

Look at your Flight Plan from Session Two. Are you the same you today? Take a moment to appreciate the ways you have grown over the last four months. If there are things you said you needed to improve on that have stayed the same, you should give deep consideration to why you're stuck. This could be important information for working through this session's Flight Plan.

1) Give your guidebook to five other people to answer the question: What can you rely on me for?

1] _____

2] _____

3] _____

4] _____

5] _____

2) Now, using your Top Five as a starting point, write out what you wish your Top Ten would look like (including making changes to your Top Five. See page 107 for the full list of strengths):

1] _____ 2] _____ 3] _____ 4] _____ 5] _____

6] _____ 7] _____ 8] _____ 9] _____ 10] _____

3) Write out an exhaustive list of all of your complaints in life, even (or perhaps especially) if you are unaccustomed to focusing on the negative.

_____

_____

_____

_____

_____

_____

_____

_____

_____

_____

4) Review your list of complaints. Look for themes. Look for opportunities. What can you do directly to affect these complaints as you head into Session Three?

_____

_____

_____

_____

_____

_____

5) If someone else who knew everything that I did, but didn't have any of my same concerns or complaints, were to give me one piece of advice, what would it be?

_____

_____

_____

_____

6) Do any recent critiques suggest a theme of something that I should be trying to improve? If yes, write that here:

_____

_____

_____

_____

7) Which parts of my work style or the way I communicate make the people around me better, smarter, or stronger?

_____

_____

_____

_____

8) Motivators — What in my life or work environment motivates and excites me?

_____

_____

_____

_____

9) Stressors — What are the things that stress me out or take a lot of energy from me?

_____

_____

_____

_____

Congratulations! You have almost completed this step in the process. All that is left is to transcribe the information on this worksheet to your Flight Plan on the next page and then carry that information with you and use it to communicate with the people in your life for the coming session.

Don't forget to . . . _FUEL UP_. Share your plan with the people in your life who will help you get there!

MY FLIGHT PLAN

THIRD SESSION | September–December

MY MOONSHOT:

_____
_____
_____

YOU CAN RELY ON ME TO Here are a few strengths or behaviors that you can rely on me to do consistently:

_____
_____
_____

THINGS I NEED TO IMPROVE Help me by watching for these things and letting me know when I am doing them [especially in real time]:

_____
_____
_____

TOP FIVE STRENGTHS

1] _____ 2] _____ 3] _____ 4] _____ 5] _____

MY MOTIVATORS These are the things that give me energy:

_____
_____
_____
_____
_____
_____
_____
_____
_____

MY STRESSORS These are the things that drain my energy:

_____
_____
_____
_____
_____
_____
_____
_____
_____

SHARABLE FLIGHT PLAN

Your fully sharable Flight Plan! Cut this out and post it where it will matter the most! Get the people in your life involved with your Moonshot to help you achieve your personal growth goals, and to capitalize on your strengths whenever they need them!

Be sure to print legibly! When you are done, cut along the dotted line. It will fit inside a five-by-seven frame!

MY
FLIGHT
PLAN

NAME:

MY MOONSHOT:

YOU CAN RELY ON ME TO   Here are a few strengths or behaviors that you can rely on me to do consistently:

THINGS I NEED TO IMPROVE   Help me by watching for these things and letting me know when I am doing them [especially in real time]:

TOP FIVE STRENGTHS

1]   2]   3]   4]   5]

MY MOTIVATORS   These are the things that give me energy:

MY STRESSORS   These are the things that drain my energy:

SUPPORT CARDS

Based on your Flight Plan, use these cards to get support from the people around you. These can be passed out in meetings, given to team members to keep, or stuck on your refrigerator at home.

PLEASE SUPPORT ME
Watch out for me and let me know if I do this:

This is the benefit I hope to gain:

PLEASE SUPPORT ME
Watch out for me and let me know if I do this:

This is the benefit I hope to gain:

PLEASE SUPPORT ME
Watch out for me and let me know if I do this:

This is the benefit I hope to gain:

PLEASE SUPPORT ME
Watch out for me and let me know if I do this:

This is the benefit I hope to gain:

PLEASE SUPPORT ME
Watch out for me and let me know if I do this:

This is the benefit I hope to gain:

PLEASE SUPPORT ME
Watch out for me and let me know if I do this:

This is the benefit I hope to gain:

PLEASE SUPPORT ME
Watch out for me and let me know if I do this:

This is the benefit I hope to gain:

PLEASE SUPPORT ME
Watch out for me and let me know if I do this:

This is the benefit I hope to gain:

CLIMBING TO THE STARS | SESSION THREE

This is where your vision becomes concrete goals. Make sure that each goal you write is measurable and directly contributes to accomplishing the goals that live further in your future. Don't forget to share these with the people in your life—sharing them makes them real and gives you a point of accountability! Another pro tip: Write these on your bathroom mirror or somewhere else that you'll see every day. If they stay in the front of your mind, you will be 1,000 times more likely to accomplish them!

MY MOONSHOT   Write its current iteration here:

_____

_____

_____

_____

_____

FIVE-YEAR GOALS   Date five years from now: _____

What two things do you need to accomplish within five years to feel comfortable you will accomplish your Moonshot?:

_____

_____

_____

_____

_____

_____

ONE-YEAR GOALS   Date one year from now: _____

What three goals do you need to accomplish within one year to feel comfortable you will accomplish your five-year goals?:

_____

_____

_____

_____

_____

_____

SESSION GOALS   Date four months from now: _____

What three things are you going to do this session to ensure you meet your one-year goals?:

_____

_____

_____

_____

_____

_____

Once you have completed this sheet, go to your calendar and add the target dates for your goals and also assign dates to accomplish the other details from your two-year vision. Also make any updates needed to the appointments you added to your calendar from your Session Two two-year vision if it has evolved while doing the Session Three work.

Don't forget to . . . *FUEL UP*. Share your plan with the people in your life who will help you get there!

WEEKLY MISSION SHEETS / / to / /

SESSION THREE GOALS

Put the same goals that you wrote in Climbing to the Stars here.

1] _____

2] _____

3] _____

WEEK 35

FOCUS 1 _____

Target a _____

Target b _____

Target c _____

FOCUS 2 _____

Target a _____

Target b _____

Target c _____

FOCUS 3 _____

Target a _____

Target b _____

Target c _____

FLIGHT PLAN FOCUS _____

_____

Target a _____

Target b _____

Target c _____

WEEK 36

FOCUS 1 _____

Target a _____

Target b _____

Target c _____

FOCUS 2 _____

Target a _____

Target b _____

Target c _____

FOCUS 3 _____

Target a _____

Target b _____

Target c _____

FLIGHT PLAN FOCUS _____

_____

Target a _____

Target b _____

Target c _____

WEEKLY MISSION SHEETS   / /   to   / /

WEEK 37

FOCUS 1 _____

Target a _____

Target b _____

Target c _____

FOCUS 2 _____

Target a _____

Target b _____

Target c _____

FOCUS 3 _____

Target a _____

Target b _____

Target c _____

FLIGHT PLAN FOCUS _____

_____

Target a _____

Target b _____

Target c _____

WEEK 38

FOCUS 1 _____

Target a _____

Target b _____

Target c _____

FOCUS 2 _____

Target a _____

Target b _____

Target c _____

FOCUS 3 _____

Target a _____

Target b _____

Target c _____

FLIGHT PLAN FOCUS _____

_____

Target a _____

Target b _____

Target c _____

NOTES Did you hit all of your targets last week? If not, diagnose it below and plan accordingly for this week!

Week 35] _____

Week 36] _____

Week 37] _____

Week 38] _____

WEEKLY MISSION SHEETS   / /   to   / /

Put the same goals that you wrote in Climbing to the Stars here.

1] _____

2] _____

3] _____

WEEK 39

FOCUS 1 _____

Target a _____

Target b _____

Target c _____

FOCUS 2 _____

Target a _____

Target b _____

Target c _____

FOCUS 3 _____

Target a _____

Target b _____

Target c _____

FLIGHT PLAN FOCUS _____

Target a _____

Target b _____

Target c _____

WEEK 40

FOCUS 1 _____

Target a _____

Target b _____

Target c _____

FOCUS 2 _____

Target a _____

Target b _____

Target c _____

FOCUS 3 _____

Target a _____

Target b _____

Target c _____

FLIGHT PLAN FOCUS _____

Target a _____

Target b _____

Target c _____

WEEKLY MISSION SHEETS   / /   to   / /

WEEK 41

FOCUS 1 _____

Target a _____

Target b _____

Target c _____

FOCUS 2 _____

Target a _____

Target b _____

Target c _____

FOCUS 3 _____

Target a _____

Target b _____

Target c _____

FLIGHT PLAN FOCUS _____

_____

Target a _____

Target b _____

Target c _____

WEEK 42

FOCUS 1 _____

Target a _____

Target b _____

Target c _____

FOCUS 2 _____

Target a _____

Target b _____

Target c _____

FOCUS 3 _____

Target a _____

Target b _____

Target c _____

FLIGHT PLAN FOCUS _____

_____

Target a _____

Target b _____

Target c _____

NOTES Did you hit all of your targets last week? If not, diagnose it below and plan accordingly for this week!

Week 39] _____

Week 40] _____

Week 41] _____

Week 42] _____

_____

WEEKLY MISSION SHEETS

SESSION THREE GOALS

Put the same goals that you wrote in Climbing to the Stars here.

1] _____

2] _____

3] _____

WEEK 43

FOCUS 1 _____

Target a _____

Target b _____

Target c _____

FOCUS 2 _____

Target a _____

Target b _____

Target c _____

FOCUS 3 _____

Target a _____

Target b _____

Target c _____

FLIGHT PLAN FOCUS _____

_____

Target a _____

Target b _____

Target c _____

WEEK 44

FOCUS 1 _____

Target a _____

Target b _____

Target c _____

FOCUS 2 _____

Target a _____

Target b _____

Target c _____

FOCUS 3 _____

Target a _____

Target b _____

Target c _____

FLIGHT PLAN FOCUS _____

_____

Target a _____

Target b _____

Target c _____

WEEKLY MISSION SHEETS   / / to / /

WEEK 45

FOCUS 1 _____

Target a _____

Target b _____

Target c _____

FOCUS 2 _____

Target a _____

Target b _____

Target c _____

FOCUS 3 _____

Target a _____

Target b _____

Target c _____

FLIGHT PLAN FOCUS _____

_____

Target a _____

Target b _____

Target c _____

WEEK 46

FOCUS 1 _____

Target a _____

Target b _____

Target c _____

FOCUS 2 _____

Target a _____

Target b _____

Target c _____

FOCUS 3 _____

Target a _____

Target b _____

Target c _____

FLIGHT PLAN FOCUS _____

_____

Target a _____

Target b _____

Target c _____

NOTES Did you hit all of your targets last week? If not, diagnose it below and plan accordingly for this week!

Week 43] _____

Week 44] _____

Week 45] _____

Week 46] _____

WEEKLY MISSION SHEETS   / / to / /

1] _____

2] _____

3] _____

WEEK 47

FOCUS 1 _____

Target a _____

Target b _____

Target c _____

FOCUS 2 _____

Target a _____

Target b _____

Target c _____

FOCUS 3 _____

Target a _____

Target b _____

Target c _____

FLIGHT PLAN FOCUS _____

Target a _____

Target b _____

Target c _____

WEEK 48

FOCUS 1 _____

Target a _____

Target b _____

Target c _____

FOCUS 2 _____

Target a _____

Target b _____

Target c _____

FOCUS 3 _____

Target a _____

Target b _____

Target c _____

FLIGHT PLAN FOCUS _____

Target a _____

Target b _____

Target c _____

WEEKLY MISSION SHEETS   / /   to   / /

WEEK 49

FOCUS 1 _____

Target a _____

Target b _____

Target c _____

FOCUS 2 _____

Target a _____

Target b _____

Target c _____

FOCUS 3 _____

Target a _____

Target b _____

Target c _____

FLIGHT PLAN FOCUS _____

_____

Target a _____

Target b _____

Target c _____

WEEK 50

FOCUS 1 _____

Target a _____

Target b _____

Target c _____

FOCUS 2 _____

Target a _____

Target b _____

Target c _____

FOCUS 3 _____

Target a _____

Target b _____

Target c _____

FLIGHT PLAN FOCUS _____

_____

Target a _____

Target b _____

Target c _____

NOTES Did you hit all of your targets last week? If not, diagnose it below and plan accordingly for this week!

Week 47] _____

Week 48] _____

Week 49] _____

Week 50] _____

WEEKLY MISSION SHEETS   /   /   to   /   /

WEEK 51

FOCUS 1 _____

Target a _____

Target b _____

Target c _____

FOCUS 2 _____

Target a _____

Target b _____

Target c _____

FOCUS 3 _____

Target a _____

Target b _____

Target c _____

FLIGHT PLAN FOCUS _____

_____

Target a _____

Target b _____

Target c _____

WEEK 52

FOCUS 1 _____

Target a _____

Target b _____

Target c _____

FOCUS 2 _____

Target a _____

Target b _____

Target c _____

FOCUS 3 _____

Target a _____

Target b _____

Target c _____

FLIGHT PLAN FOCUS _____

_____

Target a _____

Target b _____

Target c _____

NOTES Did you hit all of your targets last week? If not, diagnose it below and plan accordingly for this week!

Week 51] _____

_____

Week 52] _____

_____

CONGRATULATIONS,
VISIONAUT

END OF THE YEAR
BUT NOT YOUR
VOYAGE

Another year is gone! Before you resume your journey, spend some real time considering the work you've done in your life over the past months. This is an opportunity to get complete with your successes and failures.

Did I accomplish each of my Session Three goals? If not, why not? Remember to take full responsibility!

_____
_____
_____
_____

What could I have done differently over the last four months to get even better results than I did? Did I miss any opportunities?

_____
_____
_____
_____

What are all the things, specifically, that I have achieved in my life over the last four months (including non-Moonshot pursuits)?

_____
_____
_____
_____

Look back at your Session Three Flight Plan. How have I taken advantage of my strengths? How have I improved myself?

_____
_____
_____
_____

Think about the Support Cards that you have passed out over the past four months. How have the people in my life contributed, specifically, to my growth?

_____
_____
_____

Did I accomplish each of my one-year goals? If not, why not?

_____
_____
_____

Reread your Ready to Launch note that you wrote to yourself at the beginning of the year. What stands out? How are you different than the person who wrote that letter? How are you the same?

_____
_____
_____

Looking back at the past year, what are you most proud of?

_____
_____
_____

Looking back at the past year, what are you least proud of?

_____
_____
_____

What will you do about that previous answer?

_____
_____
_____

Are you building a life you love? Why or why not?

_____
_____
_____

We need you! Please send along any new suggestions you have accumulated or any other comments or questions that you have to moonshot@biggby.com—and—**please send us a picture of this page!** Knowing how our BIGGBY family members and fellow Visionauts have faired—good and bad—will powerfully influence the work we are doing every day to support the people around us in building a life they love!

Most importantly: Please visit biggby.com/lyla or scan the QR code to take the Life You Love Assessment! It is an opportunity to take stock of where you are in your life, look for growth opportunities, and provide us with data we can use to reinvest in the people of BIGGBY Nation.

MOONSHOT DASHBOARD

Keep track of the Moonshots of the people in your life—you are a crucial part of them achieving their dreams!

Name: _____ Date: _____

Their Moonshot:

_____

_____

_____

Name: _____ Date: _____

Their Moonshot:

_____

_____

_____

Name: _____ Date: _____

Their Moonshot:

_____

_____

_____

Name: _____ Date: _____

Their Moonshot:

_____

_____

_____

Name: _____ Date: _____

Their Moonshot:

_____

_____

_____

Name: _____ Date: _____

Their Moonshot:

_____

_____

_____

Name: _____ Date: _____

Their Moonshot:

_____

_____

_____

_____

Name: _____ Date: _____

Their Moonshot:

_____

_____

_____

_____

Name: _____ Date: _____

Their Moonshot:

_____

_____

_____

_____

Name: _____ Date: _____

Their Moonshot:

_____

_____

_____

_____

Name: _____ Date: _____

Their Moonshot:

_____

_____

_____

_____

Name: _____ Date: _____

Their Moonshot:

_____

_____

_____

_____

Name: _____ Date: _____
Their Moonshot:

_____

_____

_____

_____

Name: _____ Date: _____
Their Moonshot:

_____

_____

_____

_____

Name: _____ Date: _____
Their Moonshot:

_____

_____

_____

_____

Name: _____ Date: _____
Their Moonshot:

_____

_____

_____

_____

Name: _____ Date: _____
Their Moonshot:

_____

_____

_____

_____

Name: _____ Date: _____
Their Moonshot:

_____

_____

_____

_____

KNOWING YOUR STRENGTHS
MAKES YOU STRONGER

We believe that being very clear about what you're good at helps you to bring even more goodness.
Take the Clifton StrengthsFinder test online to determine which of these are in your Top Five.

Strengths list by Gallup CliftonStrengths and definitions by Jeremy DeRuiter.

Achiever	They are driven and LOVE checking things off their to-do list. Even on vacation.
Activator	They go from question to decision to action in 4.2 seconds. Impatience is a strength!
Adaptability	No plan? No problem! They are up for whatever, whenever!
Analytical	They love digging through details to find the why. The CIA, CPAs, and CSI all love analysts!
Arranger	Need someone to organize your closet, plan a wedding, or fix a budget? Find an arranger!
Belief	They see the world through the lens of their belief—it's the why behind much that they do.
Command	Parachute them into an emergency—they'll take over and see that stuff gets done!
Communication	They winningly weave words together without worry of woosing—ahem, losing—their audience.
Competition	They work hard because they won't be satisfied with second place. More Hermione than Ron.
Connectedness	No matter the belief system, they are comforted to know that things happen for a reason.
Consistency	This is the person you want in charge of enforcing rules evenly—making exceptions huuuurts them.
Context	They want to know how something fits into the bigger picture and are great at framing up ideas.
Deliberative	They weigh *all* of the consequences before making a decision. Shopping sprees are *not* their thing.
Developer	They have X-ray vision. They know what you're capable of even if you don't, and they love getting you there.
Discipline	They have things tightened down like a drill instructor. There is a time and place for everything.
Empathy	It might not always be enjoyable, but they easily sponge up the feelings of everyone around them.
Focus	They're born with blinders. When it's crunch time, they zero in and focus on what matters most right now.
Futuristic	You'll often find them staring off into space, merrily dreaming about what might be.
Harmony	They are peacemakers who pull people together to get best results. Argument makes them itchy.
Ideation	Light bulbs go off and confetti flies every time they think of a new idea or figure out how one connects to another.
Includer	They're the mama goose of the group who's watching out for everyone—no outcasts here, all are welcome!
Individualization	They celebrate the quirks that make you you and are great matchmakers in work or life.
Input	Adding new bits to their collection, whether new words or commemorative spoons, brings them joy.
Intellection	Losing themselves in thought is their favorite activity. They gleefully wrestle challenging ideas to the ground.
Learner	It's the journey, not the destination, that excites them. Whether they can use it or not, they love learning new things.
Maximizer	The polishers of people—they know what you're capable of and will push you to get there.
Positivity	Perhaps the most visible of the strengths—they brim with smiling energy and an optimistic worldview.
Relator	They're happiest when looking deep into the eyes (souls?) of the people around them and talking about life.
Responsibility	They walk their talk. If they say they'll do it, they will do everything in their power to see that it gets done.
Restorative	They see problems like they're highlighted in neon. Rely on them to find blind spots in your thinking.
Self-Assurance	It looks like they've read the book of life and know what's on the next page. They proceed with confidence.
Significance	They want the spotlight and to be known for who they are and what they do. #trending
Strategic	They can play out the possibilities in mind before making a move, in life or in a game. More Tyrion than Jaime.
Woo	Socially extroverted, they thrive in environments that make a wallflower faint and are excellent networkers.

NOTES

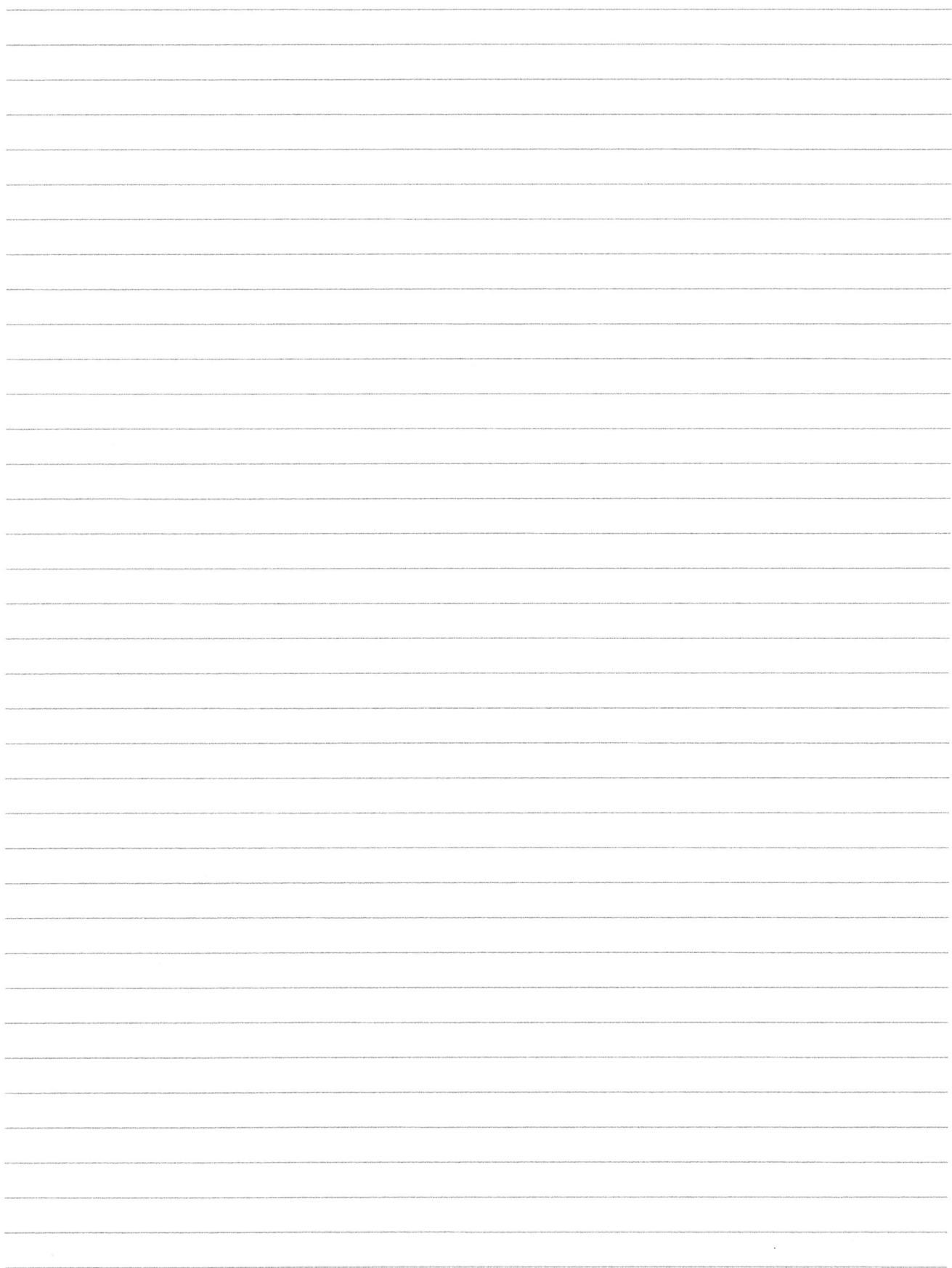

SUGGESTIONS

Do you have ideas that will help us improve this guidebook for future generations of Visionauts? Jot them down here and share them with us at moonshot@biggby.com at the end of each session. Thank you in advance for investing in the growth of the Moonshot community!

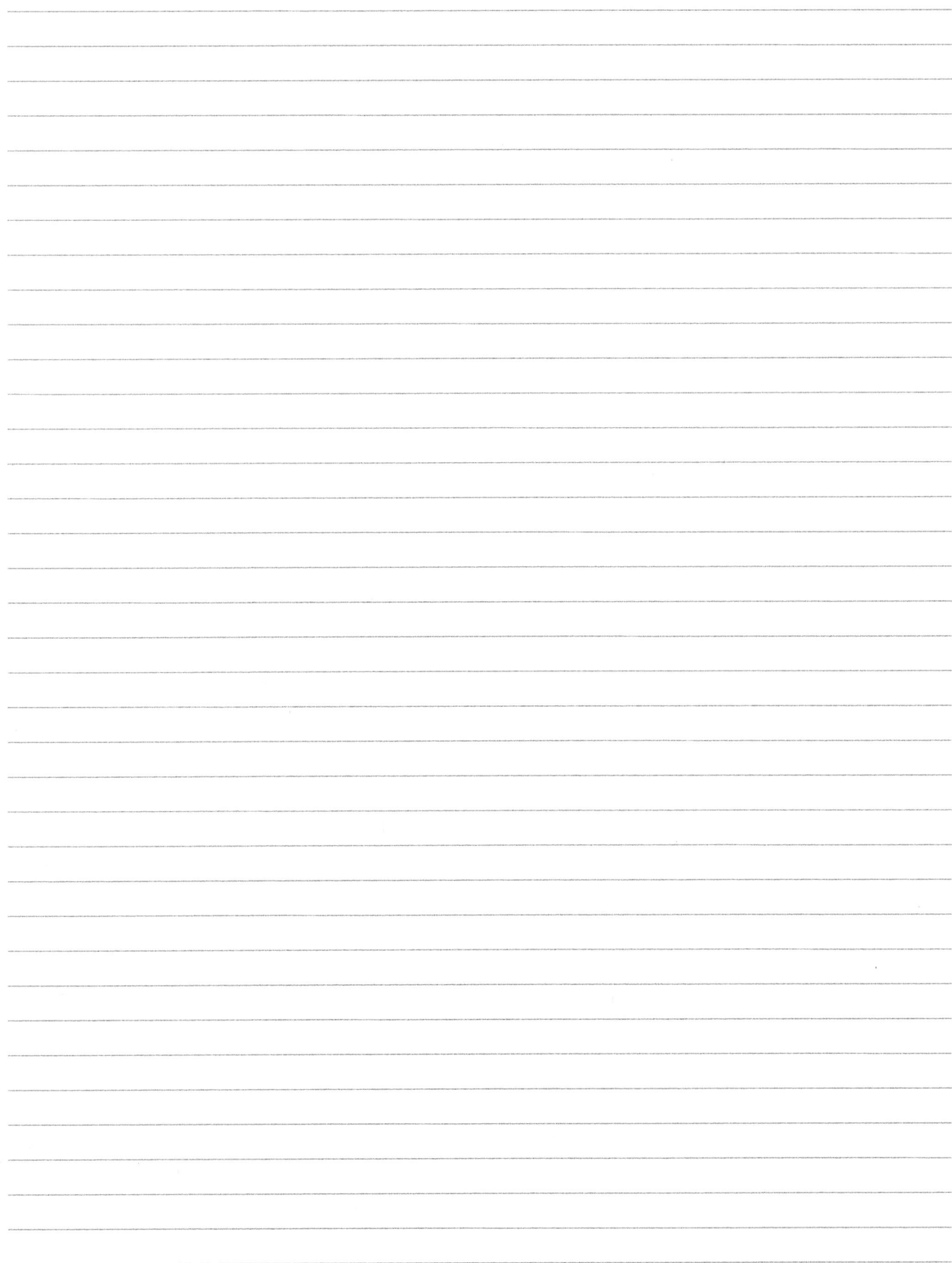

You made it. Whether this is your first time using this tool or your fiftieth, it is always going to be our hope that you uncovered something amazing as you went through it.

Special thanks for contributions:

Abby Bartshe, Adam Lawrence, Alexander McCobin, Alisha Beck, Amanda Kathryn Roman, Amanda Schreyer, Andrea Yahr, Beth Dadd, Bob Fish, Brie Roper, Caitlin Tierney, Chelsea Burrows, Christy Bui, Clark Ruper, Corey Blake, Dan Widmayer, Dante Petrarca, Dustyn Wynecoop, Emma Hickey, Emma Scott, Erica MacLeod, Glenn Meier, Heather Maynard, Heather Stevenson, Ian Sanwald, Jamie Stepanian-Bennett, Joe Kubicek, Kaliene Law, Karen Lynch-Hoag, Katrina Lafferty, Keegan Piro, Kevin Kren, Kristin Westberg, Laura Eich, Lily Hare, MaryAnne MacIntosh, Michael McFall, Nathan Havey, Nikki Robertson, Peggy Rector, Rebecca Vacek, Richard Zuniga, Samantha Lischefski, Sarah Stark, Stacey Friends, Stephanie Schlichter, Sunny DiMartino, and Tony DiPietro.

ELEVATE HUMANITY THROUGH BUSINESS.

Conscious Capitalism, Inc., supports a global community of business leaders dedicated to elevating humanity through business via their demonstration of purpose beyond profit, the cultivation of conscious leadership and culture throughout their entire ecosystem, and their focus on long-termism by prioritizing stakeholder orientation instead of shareholder primacy. We provide mid-market executives with innovative learning exchanges, transformational storytelling training, and inspiring conference experiences all designed to level-up their business operations and collectively demonstrate capitalism as a powerful force for good when practiced consciously.

We invite you, either as an individual or as a business, to join us and contribute your voice. Learn more about the global movement at www.consciouscapitalism.org.

CONSCIOUS CAPITALISM®

www.ingramcontent.com/pod-product-compliance
Lightning Source LLC
Chambersburg PA
CBHW040146200326
41519CB00035B/7606